Rossella Menegazzo

Japan

TRAVEL **COOL**TURE | Be in the know

The Aesthetics of Silence

There are so many ways to discover Japan. We could even say that there are many Japans, such is the fascination this culture has instilled in foreigners from all over the world, on different levels.

Japan has entered our homes through food, fashion, and technology, but also through nearly opposite images, ranging from cherry blossoms to social alienation.

The phenomenon of Japanism spread throughout Europe in the nineteenth century, in the wake of the Universal Exhibitions and the exportation of many artistic goods, which formed the world's most important museums and Asian art collections. Traditions, objects, and customs were brought into the homes of the European bourgeoisie; yet at the same time they brought about a more profound change, offering a different approach to reality, which artists such as Van Gogh, Manet, Monet, Degas, Toulouse-Lautrec, and Gallé skillfully incorporated into their works.

← A Buddhist monk with his hands together in the gesture of greeting and prayer

Lacquers, porcelain ware, screens and fans, kimonos, picture scrolls, polychrome prints, and hand-painted photographs are all part of the artistic artifacts that reflect the quality of Japanese craftsmanship, which seems to embody the perfect balance between humans and nature. From that era not only do we still conjure up images of samurai and geishas, but also Katsushika Hokusai's *Great Wave off Kanagawa*, which has become a universal icon, reinterpreted and cited in contemporary works, as well as transformed into pop art on all kinds of gadgets, from mugs to T-shirts, and in graffiti on walls and shutters in cities around the world. In the 1960s, there was a new Japanese wave, in the wake of Daisetsu Suzuki's lessons in the Zen philosophy in America, which stimulated first American artists and then European ones to reveal the gesture at the center of the artistic activity, with a preference for ink and paper, asymmetry, and new formal balances, while, in the seventies and eighties, Japan monopolized television schedules all over the world, being the main protagonist in the production and dissemination of manga and animated series.

The generations that unknowingly grew up with characters created in Japan, such as Heidi and Remi, Conan and Lady Oscar, Captain Harlock, Goldrake, Tranzor Z, Lupin, Sanpei, and Doraemon, are the same that today raise their children on the wave of their nostalgia for those images, often reproposed in reinterpreted versions and temporary exhibitions, contributing to the success of new animated works made for the cinema—like those by Hayao Miyazaki and Studio Ghibli—and the world of video games, not to mention manga series and literature that has never been translated before.

The hope is that this book will offer traveling readers ideas for better understanding what they encounter, as well as the desire to see and discover more, perhaps as they pass through rice fields, hills, metropolises, and ancient villages on a bullet train, catching a glimpse of the sacred Mount Fuji through the window.

→ Katsushika Hokusai, *Laughing Demoness*, from the series *One Hundred Ghost Stories*, polychrome wood-block print, 1831–32

The Aesthetics of Silence

This book, which is a far cry from a classic guide, describes Japan in a way that shows exactly what makes it such a unique place.

Those who love traveling have a desire to discover the culture of a place, the legendary stories that have made it great, just like the ones you will find in each chapter of this book.

9	**The Land of the Gods:** **From Animism to State Religion**
19	**Poems and Famous Sites:** **The Mirror Seasons of the Human Heart**
31	**A Journey Through the Capitals:** **From Kyoto to Edo, the Seats of Power**
41	**Zen:** **Paths of Meditation**
53	**Theater and Dance:** **Discipline and Performance**

63	**Eating with the Eyes**
93	**Not Just Kimonos:** **From Fashion Streets to Catwalks**
105	**Protagonists and Places of Contemporary Art**
117	**Japan As It Appears in Literature and Films**
127	**Manga and Anime: Images of Old and New Worlds**
139	**The Other Face of Japan:** *Pachinko* **and** *Karaoke*
149	**Hiroshima, Nagasaki, and Fukushima**

The Land of the Gods: From Animism to State Religion

From *Kojiki*:

Then Ama-terasu-ō-mi-kami [...] said from within: "Because I have shut myself in, I thought that Takama-no-hara would be dark, and that the Central Land of the Reed Plains would be completely dark. But why is it that Ame-no-uzume sings and dances, and all the eight-hundred myriad deities laugh?" Then Ame-no-uzume said: "We rejoice and dance because there is here a deity superior to you." [...] Ame-no-ko-yane-no-mikoto and Futo-dama-no-mikoto brought out the mirror and showed it to Ama-terasu-ō-mi-kami. Then Ama-terasu-ō-mi-kami, thinking this more and more strange, gradually came out of the door [...]. When Ama-terasu-ō-mi-kami came forth, Takama-no-hara and the Central Land of the Reed Plains of themselves became light.

← *Koinobori* means "carp streamer" and they are in fact large paper or fabric windsocks in the form of a carp (*koi*), flown on poles on "Children's Day" (*kodomo no hi*), which is celebrated on 5 May

Japan is one of the most sought-after destinations in the world, and its culture continues to fascinate not only the West, but also Asian countries, overcoming language barriers through products which stand out for their simplicity and intimate connection with nature. Everything in Japan is divine—from Mount Fuji to rice—and this is where we need to start from to understand it all.

It is said that there are seven gods in each grain of rice, and this is why children are taught to pick out every single grain of rice from their bowl with their chopsticks. But it appears that in Japan the divine also resides in turnip tops, and in every single blade of grass in the universe. Those of you who have seen Hayao Miyazaki's animated film *My Neighbor Totoro* will have grasped this concept well, between the scenes of the old house, with its wooden beams which squeak to make themselves heard, and those in which black balls of soot take possession of uninhabited nooks and crannies.

The term *Kami*, often followed by the honorific suffix *sama*, refers to deities, gods, spirits, and protective deities. The same character, using the alternate reading *shin*, composes the word *shintō*, the "Way of the Gods." Another word that derives from this character is *kamikaze*, which means "divine wind." Since World War II, it has been associated with suicide attacks carried out against the enemy by pilots and their planes, in the name of the emperor, considered a descendant of the gods. Actually, the term was coined to honor the 1281 typhoon that destroyed the Mongol fleet that was preparing to attack the southern coast of Japan, as the typhoon was perceived to be divine intervention.

The *Kojiki*

Shintoism was only codified as an indigenous religious system in 712, with the compilation of the *Kojiki (An Account of Ancient Matters)*, arising from the need to respond to the arrival of religious and philosophical thoughts from the Asian continent in Japan, such as Buddhism, Taoism, and Confucianism. The text records pre-existing rituals and cults which were practiced within families and peasant villages; it affirms the intrinsic pantheistic belief in the creation of Yamato, an ancient name for Japan, according to which the creator gods Izanagi and Izanami and all creation, men, women, animals, animate and inanimate beings in nature, are of equal importance; finally, it asserts the sacred nature of the emperor, in that he is a direct descendant of the *kami* from whom he received the three sacred objects: the sword (value), the mirror (wisdom), and the *magatama* jewel (benevolence). The belief that the imperial figure was a divine being only ended in January 1946, when Emperor Hirohito himself—on the insistence of American authorities—declared that the emperor was in fact a human being in a radio broadcast, the second he had made since Japan was defeated in August 1945.

The Great Sun Goddess Amaterasu Ōmikami is the main deity in the *Kojiki*, and the story of the cave is linked to her: offended by the actions of her brother Susanoo, God of storms, the goddess decides to hide in a cave, causing the land of Yamato to plunge into darkness. Amaterasu was enticed to peek out of the cave by the shamanic dance of the goddess Amenouzume, the song of the birds, and the cunning use of a mirror that reflected her own image, leading her to believe that there was a goddess more beautiful than herself, thereby restoring light to Japan: that is, the entire world.

Sacred Signs

Those arriving in Japan will immediately start seeing small signs indicating special places linked to the presence of deities, as they look out of the train window on the journey from the airport to the cities: centuries-old trees, perhaps weather-beaten, with twisted straw ropes (*shimenawa*) wrapped around their trunks, adorned with zigzag-shaped paper streamers (*shide*) reminiscent of lightning, symbolizing the union between the earth and the sky, and the rain that fertilizes the soil and guarantees subsistence; or small altars in the form of a shrine on the edges of rice fields, or at crossroads, on which passers-by leave offerings such as rice, oranges, and sake. These are decorated with traditional Shinto elements, both architectural and ritualistic: the *torii*, the entrance gate to the sacred area, composed of two tall pillars connected by a horizontal crossbar, both ends of which curve up toward the sky; and the *shimenawa*, the rope hanging above the entrance gate.

The God Inari and the *Kitsune* Fox

Shintō gods were not depicted visually, although in some shrines (*jinja*) you may find statues of a sitting fox, of various sizes, with a bushy tail attached to its body. This is Inari, the God of rice and bountiful harvests: an ancient cult that probably arose from the villagers' fear of the slyness of the fox and its nocturnal intrusions into the rice fields and farm enclosures. There are many stories in which the fox (*kitsune*) is always ready to deceive wayfarers by taking on the appearance of a seductive girl or is depicted as a will-o'-the-wisp that appears on the path of those who are unfortunate. Legend says that in the evening, or when the sun shines through rain, you might see foxes holding their wedding processions (*kitsune no yomeiri*), sumptuous parades of lanterns, of which there is no trace the following day. And the fox has also been associated with the shooting stars known as *Amanokitsune* (Sky Foxes) since antiquity, perhaps because the trail is reminiscent of a fox's tail.

The Husband-and-Wife Rocks

Along the archipelago's jagged coasts, shaped by the powerful ocean that provides the primary source of livelihood for a country that relies on fishing and at the same time causes huge calamities like the tsunamis that have marked, and continue to mark, the life of Japan, you can often see particularly evocative cone-shaped rock formations jutting out of

→ Utagawa Hiroshige, *New Year's Eve Foxfires at the Changing Tree [enoki] at* [the shrine of] *Oji,* from the series One Hundred Famous Views of Edo, polychrome wood-block print, 1857

↳ A Hiroshige print from 1857, one of his *One Hundred Famous Views of Edo*. It depicts white foxes gathered under a large tree on New Year's Eve at the Oji Shrine. In 1840, Kuniyoshi painted a group of foxes being trained in disguise: some are wearing a kimono, or getting ready to put one on, while others are already disguised as a monk or a woman.

▲ "Husband-and-Wife Rocks" (*Meoto Iwa*), two rocks that are considered sacred, situated in Futami Bay, Mie Prefecture

the sea, connected by a sacred *shimenawa* rope adorned with rice straw cones and zigzag-shaped paper streamers. This is the divine that resides in every element of nature. It is possible to see many of these along the narrow strip of coastline in the northwest, from the window of the regional train that connects the Niigata region to Yamagata, but the main place is Futami Bay, Futamigaura, in the Ise Prefecture, rendered famous by Hiroshige's well-known polychrome print, part of the *Thirty-Six Views of Mount Fuji* landscape series he painted in 1858. Here there are two rocks, one of which is large and the other smaller, hence the name *meoto iwa* (the husband-and-wife rocks). They are connected by a twisted sacred rope, and there is a small *torii* on top of the large rock.

→ Katsushika Hokusai, *Tama River in Musashi Province*, from the series *Thirty-six Views of Mount Fuji*, polychrome wood-block print, c. 1830

The Sites of *Shintō*

The most symbolic place of Shintoism is Mount Fuji, the majestic volcano that stands between the prefectures of Yamanashi and Shizuoka, with a height of 12,390 ft (3,776 m). Mount Fuji is perhaps the most immortalized subject in nineteenth-century prints and paintings: Hokusai first dedicated thirty-six prints to the mountain in around 1832–34, followed by a book with one hundred views, and Hiroshige reproduced again the thirty-six views in 1856–58. In the Edo period, all Japanese people were encouraged to go on a pilgrimage to Mount Fuji at least once in their life: the mountain and its springs became a cult, and the pilgrims were called *Fujiko*. However, as women were not allowed to climb the mountain, and for many others it was too difficult to reach, little Mount Fujis (*Fujizuka*) were built inside shrines throughout the country, where one could go on a symbolic pilgrimage. There is a "Little Fuji" in Tokyo, built in 1790 in the Teppozu Inaribashi Minato Jinja shrine in Hacchobori, which became famous and is depicted in Hiroshige's series *One Hundred Famous Views of Edo* (1856–58).

Shrines: Ise, Izumo, and Meiji

There are thousands of *jinja* shrines in Japan. They are found next to the pavilions of Buddhist temples, squeezed between futuristic skyscrapers in large cities, and in villages, where they are an important part of village life, being the epicenter of festivals (the *matsuri*), processions, and dances. The *jingu* are the most important shrines, because they are directly linked to the imperial family. The first and oldest is *Ise Jingu*, in the Mie Prefecture. It dates back to the fourth century B.C. and houses the sacred mirror of Amaterasu, at the behest of the imperial princess Yamatohime, the shrine's first priestess. Starting in the seventh century, it was pulled down and rebuilt every 20 years as part of the *Shikinen Sengū*, a ritual of renewal. It involves a series of rituals and ceremonies, starting with choosing the trees to cut for the new pavilion, and ending with its inauguration in the presence of the imperial family. While it is being rebuilt, the old workers pass on their technical knowledge to the new generation, who will then pass on theirs the next time it is rebuilt, and so on. The shrine consists of two complexes: the inner shrine (*naiku*), an area of about 13,590 acres (5,500 hectares) surrounded by a high wooden fence, with several sober stilted pavilions made of cypress wood, where the Goddess of the Sun Amaterasu resides and which is closed to the public; and the outer shrine (*geku*), open to pilgrims, which extends into the cypress forest and contains one hundred and twenty-five smaller shrines, where the main deity is Toyouke Omikami, guardian of food, clothing, and housing.

On the west coast of Shimane Prefecture stands another large shrine, Izumo Taisha, which Japan's first annals in the eighth century record as the tallest wooden building of the time. Today's shrine is smaller, but it has the biggest *shimenawa* in Japan: it is 44 ft (13.5 m) long and is one of the most beautiful examples of simple Japanese craftsmanship. The shrine is said to have been donated to Ōkuninushi, believed to be the first ruler of the earthly world, by the goddess Amaterasu, as a sign of gratitude for having agreed

↑ Izumo Grand Shrine (*Izumo Taisha*) with the largest sacred rope (*shimenawa*) in Japan, in Shimane Prefecture

to cede the country to his nephew Ninigi no Mikoto when he stepped down to rule the spirit world. Ōkuninushi, God of love bonds (*en-musubi*), is in fact the main deity worshipped at the shrine; many couples go there to leave their names and wishes before marrying, writing them on sheets of paper and tying (*musubu*) them to tree branches and fences in the shrine.

In the heart of Tokyo, between the luxury shopping street of Omotesando and the young fashion district of Harajuku, there is also an evergreen forest that attracts both residents and tourists alike: the *Meiji Jingu*, the Grand Shrine built and inaugurated in 1920, dedicated to Mutsuhito, the emperor who marked the Meiji period, and to the consort Shōken, on the throne from 1867 to 1912. The exhibition of the imperial collection of chrysanthemums held there every November on the occasion of the culture festival is well-known.

Poems and Famous Sites: The Mirror Seasons of the Human Heart

"But aside from house and family, it is nature that gives me the most pleasure: the changes through the seasons, the blossoms and leaves of autumn and spring, the shifting patterns of the skies. People have always debated the relative merits of the groves of spring and the fields of autumn, and had trouble coming to a conclusion."

– Murasaki Shikibu, The Tale of Genji

← Utagawa Hiroshige II, *Yoshino Mountain in the Yamato Province,* from the series *One Hundred Famous Views in the Various Provinces,* polychrome woodblock print, 1859

"The Shining Prince" Genji—the epitome of sophistication and elegance, hero of the first great novel of Japanese literature, written in around 1008 by Murasaki Shikibu, a lady-in-waiting at the Imperial court—said that everyone has one season that is in tune with their personality, and no one can ever convince them otherwise. This is why in Japan, everyday life, places, fashion and food, paintings and poems are marked by the colors and rhythms of the seasons.

Ancient imperial anthologies of *waka* poetry, like the *Man'yōshū (Collection of Ten Thousand Leaves)* and the *Kokin waka shū (Collection of Ancient and Modern Japanese Poems)*, are centered around feelings toward nature and changes in nature, and this is why the poems are divided into seasonal sections (*shiki*). In both classical Japanese *waka* poetry and the later *haiku*—short poems that reflect on the key elements of Zen Buddhism. The reference is, above all, to the season, and this is done through the evocation of specific keywords (*kigo*), such as an element of nature, an insect, a flower, the name of a river, or a mountain, or a more universal sensation such as a smell, a color, or a sound.

To understand this deep connection, it is enough to read the preface to Ki no Tsurayuki's Collection of Ancient and Modern Japanese Poems:

"Japanese poetry has the human heart as seed and myriads of words as leaves. It comes into being when men use the seen and the heard to give voice to feelings aroused by the innumerable events in their lives. The song of the warbler among the blossoms, the voice of the frog dwelling in the water—these teach us that every living creature sings. It is song that moves heaven and earth without effort, stirs emotions in the invisible spirits and gods, brings harmony to the relations between men and women, and calms the hearts of fierce warriors."

— Ki no Tsurayuki (edited by Ikuko Sagiyama), *Kokin waka shū. Collection of ancient and modern Japanese poems.*

The four seasons and the minuscule changes in nature dictate the subjects of poetry and paintings, becoming an expression of human feelings like a mirror. This pathos of things is called *mono no aware*, and is what moves the human soul and every area of creation.

Places That are Famous for a Season

In paintings, the seasonal keywords that are often used in poetry are transformed into views of places that have become famous (*meisho*) precisely because of the association with elements related to the beauty and lure of nature; sometimes they are inspired by poetry itself, transcribing it until it is incorporated into the painting. Although at first glance it would appear that the landscapes on the panels of a screen are simply a realistic painting of a panorama, this is not the case. If you look carefully at the flowers, plants, and animals, you can in fact see the seasons slowly changing as you move from the first panels on the right to the left: spring is depicted with flowering pink and white cherry trees and new, bright green grass; summer with elongated leaves on willow trees and fireflies on a hot evening; fall can be recognized by the reddening of the maple leaves and flocks of wild ducks flying across a full moon; while in winter there is a camellia peeking through the snow and the symbolic bamboo, pine, and plum, known as "the three friends of winter" because of their hardiness, as well as the fact that the plum tree is the first to announce the arrival of spring with its buds.

Then there is an image linked to certain places or locations which are particularly beautiful in a given season: places handed down from literature to painting, which the Japanese, and also many tourists, recognize as the best place to be in that season.

Spring

At the beginning of each year, a cherry-blossom forecast is added to the weather forecast, which announces, region by region, the dates when the trees will start to flower, and when they will reach full bloom, also recommending the best spots in the cities or prefectures for an outdoor picnic or a walk under the clouds of petals. The *meisho* in Kyoto that are the most mentioned in poetry and depicted in paintings—on lacquer-ware and pottery, in the polychrome wood-block prints by *Ukiyo-e* masters like Hokusai and Hiroshige, and in nineteenth century hand-colored photographs—include: Mount Yoshino, with its rounded, gentle top covered in a blanket of cherry trees; the Arashiyama district, where the banks of the river Katsura are adorned with cherry blossoms reflected in the water, which can be admired from the wooden boats that go down the river, or from the panoramic train (*torokko densha*) that crosses the valley and takes tourists up to the village of Sagano; and the Kiyomizu-dera temple, in the heart of the city, whose terrace offers one of the most beautiful spring views of the gardens and surrounding forest dotted with cherry trees. There are also many famous views in Tokyo, which since the time it was still called Edo have been depicted in prints of the floating world, and in nineteenth-century photographs taken in spring. One of the most popular places for a walk or a picnic is Ueno Park (*Ueno kōen*), home to

several major art museums, the city zoo, and the Shinobazu pond, which is covered with lotus flowers; in the past, *ricksho* (rickshaws) took young women in kimonos through the park to enjoy the cherry blossoms. The Yoyogi kōen, Shinjuku gyoen, Inokashira, and Hibiya kōen parks are also very popular today, as are the gardens surrounding the Imperial Palace and Chidorigafuchi, where you can admire the cherry blossoms on the moat around the imperial walls in Kudanshita (also at night, thanks to the specially designed lighting). The Musashi Koganei area is a historic spot for admiring the row of cherry trees along the banks of the river, which became famous thanks to Hiroshige and Hokusai's prints and is still very popular today, as is—also with the Japanese—a walk along the canal in the heart of the elegant district of Meguro, or through the cemeteries of Aoyama and Yanaka, which in spring turn into gardens.

↑ Katsushika Hokusai, *Togetsu Bridge at Arashiyama in Yamashiro Province*, from the series *Unusual Views of Famous Bridges in Various Provinces*, polychrome wood-block print, 1834
← Cherry blossoms on Mount Yoshino, near Kyoto

Due to its very short life, the cherry tree blossom is a symbol of the transience of human life, so much so that, as literature suggests, a sensitive person appreciates a tree whose petals are beginning to fall more than one in full bloom. The cherry blossom is also the symbol of the samurai spirit.

*If there were
no cherry blossoms
in this world,
How much more tranquil
our hearts would be in spring*

— Kokin waka shū, *I:53 Ariwara no Narihira*

Fall

While Mount Yoshino is the symbol of spring, Mount Takao symbolizes fall and is depicted in one of the first genre screens of the 16th-century Kanō school, painted by Kanō Hideyori. The painting depicts all the typical elements of a fall landscape—a river, red maple trees, a flock of flying ducks, and snow-capped peaks in the distance—with human figures engaged in activities related to the season: a group of adults and children having a picnic under the red maple trees, another group of people enjoying a show by musicians and dancers, others chatting, a passerby playing the flute on top of the bridge. Mount Takao is still a fall destination today, with a dedicated festival; and the Japanese await—as they do for the blossoming of the cherry trees—the regional forecast for the dates when the leaves of the maple trees will turn red, from region to region.

In addition to Mount Takao, another key place linked to fall is the Tatsuta River, which flows between Osaka and Nara. As a famous site (*meisho*), it is also the subject of many polychrome wood-block prints, and also of many poems, being a keyword (*kigo*) that immediately evokes fall. It

← Utagawa Hiroshige, *Koganei in Musashi Province*, from the series *Thirty-six Views of Mount Fuji*, polychrome wood-block print, 1858

↟ Red maple trees over the roofs of Jingoji Temple on Mount Takao, Kyoto

is included in Hiroshige's series of prints *Views of Famous Sites in the Sixty-odd Provinces*, and is also the subject of a colorful print in Hokusai's series *One Hundred Poets, One Poem Each Explained by the Nurse*. The print portrays the poet Ariwara no Narihira through the view of an arched bridge crossing a stream scattered with floating red maple leaves; the passers-by are country people, engaged in daily activities, while in the distance you can also see red maple trees on the mountains. Inscribed in the cartouche, there is a line from a poem by Narihira, which refers to the Tatsuta River:

Waters of Tatsuta, never even in the golden age of old did the gods in their might behold you fairer, laced with crimson of leaves.

↦ Takahashi Dōhachi III, large ceramic bowl with cherry blossom and maple leaf motif, first half of 19th century

↳ **Fall and Spring in a Bowl**
At the Metropolitan Museum in New York, there is a large ceramic bowl made by Takahashi Dōhachi III, heir to the tradition of tea master and potter Nin'ami Dōhachi (1783–1855), which depicts the symbolic images of the two seasons the Japanese love most. It is decorated with polychrome enamels, with a motif that starts from the two opposite sides and meets in the center of the bowl, dividing the space thus: on one side, a maple tree branch opens out into an array of red leaves, like a brocade (*nishiki*); on the other, a cherry tree in full bloom opens out into a cloud of white petals (*kumo*). The motif is called "cloud brocade," *kumo nishiki*, and, without actually saying so, it refers to Mount Yoshino and the Tatsuta River.

♦ Katsushika Hokusai, *Poem by Ariwara no Narihira*, from the series *One Hundred Poems Explained by the Nurse*, polychrome wood-block print, 1839

Poems and Famous Sites: The Mirror Seasons of the Human Heart

A Journey Through the Capitals: From Kyoto to Edo, the Seats of Power

"All travelers are to be closely examined. Stopping for one night is permissible, but no one at all shall be lodged for two nights."

— From the regulations issued by the Superintendent of Highways in 1686

Moving the capital from city to city, sometimes even just a few miles, is a custom originally attributable to Shintō rites related to impurity, as a place was considered impure after the death of an Emperor. Starting from the Kamakura period (1185–1333), however, the relocation of the capital became a political and administrative choice, linked to the highest shogunate military office, while Kyoto remained the Imperial capital until 1868.

← Matsumoto Castle and the Red Bridge in Nagano Prefecture

There is one genre of Japanese art that has gained more international fame than any other, by speaking to a wide audience of distant places, fashions, and customs. They are mostly unknown and sometimes incomprehensible to a geographically and culturally different world, because they are based on rules, values, and aesthetics that are a far cry from those of the West. It is called *Ukiyo-e*—which literally translates as "images of the floating world"—and it is a type of painting that uses the wood-block printing technique, while still applying the ink and paint by hand. This printing technique, imported from China in the seventeenth century and initially only done with black ink, soon evolved, leading to *Beni*-e prints, painted with red pigment obtained from safflower, and *Urushi*-e, painted with black varnish-like ink that remained glossy. This led to the creation of prints with many different colors, created by carving a separate wood block for each color, giving the impression of a silk brocade, hence the name *Nishiki*-e (brocade images).

The Edo Period

From 1603 to 1868, Japan was ruled by the samurai class (*bushi*). Edo, today's Tokyo, was chosen as the administrative capital by the first of the Tokugawa *shōguns*, a family that overcame all its rival clans—first and foremost those of the Toyotomi and Nobunaga— and which fought to unify Japan under its own rule, guaranteeing a stable military government that controlled over two hundred and sixty fiefs, each under the administration of a feudal lord with the title *daimyō*, meaning "great name." The Edo period, and consequently the shogunate, ended in 1868 with the Meiji Restoration, which restored imperial rule, although based on a Western con-

→ Ancient map of the eastern capital of Edo (today's Tokyo), polychrome wood-block print, c. 1840

stitutional model; therefore, any title or privilege linked to the samurai aristocracy was prohibited, including wearing the traditional two swords.

Over the course of one hundred years, Edo became the most populous city in the world: on the one hand, the long period of peace under the Tokugawa shogunate ended the constant state of warfare, forcing the samurai to take up jobs and trades within the new society and city institutions; and, on the other, it permitted the rise of a new merchant class, the *Chōnin*, which quickly became wealthy at the ex-

Filmography

- *Ran* (1985) directed by Akira Kurosawa
- *James Bond. You Only Live Twice* (1967) directed by Lewis Gilbert
- *The Last Samurai* (2003) directed by Edward Zwick

pense of the aristocratic class, which, although remaining in command, possessed increasingly less and had accumulated debts.

From Edo to Kyoto

In the center of the new eastern capital, Edo, far from Kyoto, which continued to be the Imperial seat, stood Edo Castle, home to the *shogun*. It was an imposing building built for defense, with several stone towers around which the residences of the *daimyō* and their servants were built in a circle. Obliged to offer tributes and reside in the capital for alternating periods of time, they traveled from their provinces in pomp and grandeur via the new large roads connecting Kyoto to Edo, which ran along the coast and through the mountains.

The scenes of these journeys are the most curious depictions in *Ukiyo-e* prints. Bird's-eye views of processions of tiny men on horseback and in litters, followed by all kinds of goods being transported in large trunks on wagons or people's backs. The figures, led by standard bearers, are portrayed crossing rivers or climbing mountain passes, stopping for the night at posthouses, removing their armor, laying down their arms, and watering the horses and eating hot food and drinking tea at restaurants and stalls along the way. But they also portrayed relaxing moments, while being entertained and captivated by the women in tea houses and inns opened especially for them.

Many of these prints were in fact dedicated to views along the two main routes, the Tōkaidō and the Kisokaidō, and they show the newly created sites as posthouses, which were necessary for journeys that lasted for weeks. On the Tōkaidō, the eastern sea road and the busiest because it was flat, there were fifty-three rest stops, or fifty-five if you also count where it started in Edo, at the Nihonbashi Bridge, and ended in Kyoto, at the Sanjō Bridge. There were sixty-nine on the Kisokaidō, a more rugged

→ Katsushika Hokusai, *Famous Places on the Tokaido Road in One View*, polychrome wood-block print, 1818

↳ **The Tōkaidō Today**
Today the old Tōkaidō stations correspond to the stations of the local train that connects Tokyo to Kyoto, a slow journey of about eight hours, but fun if you are looking for some traces of the past: a row of pine trees or cypresses; a small village of wooden houses; a small shop that has been there for centuries; a glimpse of Mount Fuji or the ocean.
Tōkaidō is also the name of the high-speed train line that the *Shinkansen* travels on between Tokyo and Kyoto, taking just over two hours. From this train you can catch a brief glimpse of the ocean on one side, and Mount Fuji on the other, clouds and mist permitting, albeit at a high speed.

road that crossed the mountains, but this is precisely why it offered glimpses of mountain gorges, streams, and beautiful snowy views.

Each posthouse gradually became associated with a characteristic, a landscape, an attraction that distinguished it, becoming part of an image of the famous sites (*meisho*) that can be considered the predecessor to the postcard, eventually even reaching us through the hand-painted albumin photography of the first photographers of the late nineteenth century. This was possible thanks to the diffusion of images created by the great masters of painting the floating world, such as Hokusai and Hiroshige, using the wood-block printing technique, of which hundreds of copies were distributed in an increasingly flourishing publishing market.

Tales of Castles

Many of the castles that can be seen in Japan today are reconstructions or reproductions of the originals, which were partly dismantled at the end of the Azuchi-Momoyama period due to many lords of the provinces losing economic power following the unification under the Tokugawa shogunate, and therefore no longer able to maintain them. Some of these castles were destroyed by the Meiji government at the end of the nineteenth century, as they were a symbol of the shogunate's power which they had to defeat, while others were bombed in World War II.

One of the most visited by tourists is Ōsaka Castle, which Toyotomi Hideyoshi started building in 1584, and was destroyed by fire in 1615 during the repeated Tokugawa attacks. The oldest part of what can be seen today dates back to 1931. Hideyoshi also had Fushimi Castle built in the Momoyama district of Kyoto, parts of which were used to build Nijō-jo Castle.

Azuchi Castle, near Lake Biwa, was built by Oda Nobunaga in around 1576–79, and destroyed in a fire in 1583; written testimonies are all that remain of its magnificence.

Himeji Castle

Himeji Castle in Hyōgo Prefecture is one of the few original castles that can still be visited. Majestic buildings were fortified to attack and defend against the firearms that arrived in Japan with the Portuguese in 1543. Today a UNESCO World Heritage Site and National Treasure of Japan, the castle was built by Ikeda Terumasa and completed by Hideyoshi in 1609, who expanded the building he had inherited from Ikeda. It is on top of a hill and stands out due to its high, slightly concave walls made of enormous stone boulders. The whiteness of the walls covered with lime and shell ash, which made it fire-resistant in the event of attacks, and the overall effect of the interlocking roof shapes, staggered gables, and apices surmounting the four fortified towers, earned the castle the nickname Shirasagijō, "White Heron Castle." It is the typical castle associated with *ninjas*: while from the outside it appears to be a five-story building, once inside visitors can see that the intricate and strategic internal construction is actually spread out over seven staggered floors, with staircases leading to rectangular windows designed for firing with a bow and arrow, and triangular ones for rifles and cannons. In Matsumoto, in the Nagano Prefecture, there is another fascinating castle with black wooden walls, known as "Crow Castle."

In Tokyo: When Edo Castle Became the Imperial Palace

Edo Castle was already the Imperial residence when it was destroyed by fire in 1873, because following the Meiji Restoration the emperor had moved from Kyoto to what would later become the city of Tokyo. Today, only the Imperial palace's eastern gardens (*kokyō gaien*) can be visited. This huge "green lung" (evergreen forest) in the heart of Tokyo extends outside the palace walls, which are built of large boulders and surrounded by a moat, and there is an expanse of pine trees which reach the surrounding area of skyscrapers that are home to finance firms, government

↪ **Legends**
Himeji Castle is associated with the legend of the ghost of Okiku, a beautiful young maid who refused to marry her master. After trying to force her hand in marriage by stealing one of the ten plates she had been entrusted with, her master killed her and threw her body down a well. In the famous *One Hundred Ghost Stories (Hyaku monogatari)* series of prints done by Hokusai in around 1830, Okiku is portrayed as a vengeful spirit: she is depicted as a female form rising out of the well, her long neck made up of plates. The story was first made into a puppet-theater show (*bunraku*) in 1741, *The Dish Mansion at Banchō (Banchō Sarayashiki)*, while the first Kabuki adaptation was staged in 1824.

offices, and communications companies. From the glass offices that now tower over the palace, you can enjoy a previously forbidden view of the park. The gardens themselves are accessed through an imposing gate and are worth visiting in any season, thanks to the beautiful cherry and maple trees, the ruins of the castle's ancient tower, and, since November 2023, the opportunity to see the masterpieces of the Imperial collections in the new museum that is open to the public.

In Kyoto: Nijō Castle

One of Japan's most elegant castles is in Kyoto. Built on a raised area of flat land (*honmaru*), it actually looks like an aristocratic wooden flatland house, and the walls and the moat surrounding the large garden are the only existing fortification. The construction of Nijō-jo began in 1569, at the behest of General Oda Nobunaga, but the original building was destroyed by fire in 1750, and what we see today is the castle built by the first *shōgun* Tokugawa Ieyasu, who went to Kyoto to receive his title from the emperor in 1603. Later, in 1626, on the occasion of Emperor Go-Mizunoo's official visit, it was modernized with the addition of a new extension, an event that was recorded in the paintings on several screens, which capture life inside and outside the imperial capital and its main attractions. The large *shoin*-style rooms are divided by sliding doors, mostly painted with bright pigments and motifs of large pines on gold-leaf backgrounds; these were made by the artists of the Kanō school, which worked for the great warlords from the 15th century onward.

← Katsushika Hokusai, *The Mansion of the Plates*, from the series *One Hundred Ghost Stories*, polychrome wood-block print, 1831–32

Zen: Paths of Meditation

"An unmatched set of bound books can be considered unattractive, but Bishop Kōyū impressed me deeply by saying that only a boring man will always want things to match; real quality lies in irregularity [...]. In all things, perfect regularity is tasteless. Something left not quite finished is very appealing, a gesture toward the future."

—Yoshida Kenkō, Tsurezuregusa (Essays in Idleness), 1330–1333

← A monk meditating in front of the *karesansui* ("dry garden") at the temple in Kyoto

Whether it is in painting, architecture, design, fashion, or meditation, anything that tends to use simple forms and materials, monochrome, or silence, is commonly associated with Zen, which Japan seems to have nailed. But what is Zen, and in which forms is it actually expressed?

Zen is one of the many schools of Buddhism that were introduced to Japan from the mainland over the centuries. Its origins seem to go back to a sermon that Buddha gave his disciples by silently holding up a flower. Only one disciple, Kāsyapa, grasped its meaning, and he handed down this teaching until—almost a thousand years later, in the sixth century—the semi-legendary Indian Buddhist monk Bodhidharma founded the *Chán* (derived from the Sanskrit word *dhyāna*, meaning "meditation") school of Chinese Buddhism, which the Japanese embraced and, in the twelfth century, translated as *zen*.

After suffering decades of internal wars between military clans, Japan had seen the collapse of imperial power, the aesthetics of its court, and the beginning of a military-type government, with the proclamation of the first *shōgun* Minamoto no Yoritomo in 1192. Zen philosophy met the needs and ethics of a warrior class that was always engaged on the battlefield and poised between life and death. Unlike other Buddhist schools, Zen Buddhism is not based on scriptures, the *sutras*, but on a disciple learning directly from a master, on personal exercise and strong daily discipline, which also included meditation to achieve detachment from trivial, illusory reality. This is why the principles of Zen, steeped in Chinese culture, were adopted in every area.

Daruma

The name Bodhidharma recalls both the state of being Awakened, Enlightened—from the Sanskrit word *bodhi* meaning "enlightenment"—and the "Law of the Buddha" of the Sanskrit *dharma*. It is therefore a name that evokes the completion of a path that through meditation allows us to understand the profound truth that lies within each of us. In Japan, Bodhidharma is also more simply called Daruma, and the image of the meditating monk sitting cross-legged with his hands folded in his lap, his palms facing outward, wearing a red robe, has not only become the subject of paintings, but also of toys and good-luck charms, which are oval-shaped as if his legs have fallen off after meditating in the sitting position (*zazen*) for so long.

→ Hakuin Ekaku, *Portrait of Daruma (Bodhidarma)*, ink on paper, vertical scroll, mid-17th century

Filmography

- Masayuki Suzuki, *Yudō*, 2022
- Hideki Takeuchi, *Thermae Romae*, 2012; *Thermae Romae II*, 2014
- Yojirō Takita, *Okuribito* (*Departures*), 2008
- Kei Kumai, *Sen no Rikyu* (*Death of a Tea Master*), 1989

His face, which many Zen monk painters draw to practice their brush and ink technique, has marked Indian features, thick eyebrows and beard, a large nose and big ear lobes, and round, wide-open eyes without eyelids, with the pupils looking in all four directions. His appearance is linked to another fascinating legend surrounding the tea tradition: the story goes that Daruma cut off his eyelids after falling asleep just once while he was meditating—so that it would never happen again; and it is said that from the fallen eyelids, the tea plant started growing. This type of tea is

known to have beneficial properties and to help you stay alert, so much so that a ceremony developed around it.

Dō: The Path

Dō is the Japanese version of *Dao/Tao*, which translates as the Way, the Art and discipline. It is the suffix that determines all the disciplines a Zen follower must practice daily to help them with their meditation. The Zen philosophy incorporates the art of calligraphy, *shodō*; the martial arts of the samurai, *budō* or *bushidō*, which includes all the other disciplines (*aikidō*, *yudō*, *judō*, etc.); the art of fragrance or incense, *kodō*; the art of flower arranging, *kadō*, better known as *Ikebana*; but also the creation and maintenance of dry gardens, *karesansui*; the performing art of *Nō* theater; and the art of tea, *sadō*, which can be said to include all the arts. In the last decade, the Way of the Bath, *yudō*, was also founded, with the aim of reassessing the tradition of public baths (*sentō*), thermal baths (*onsen*), and the private *ofuro*.

The Way of Tea

The Japanese word for the tea ceremony is *Chanoyu*, which literally means "hot water (*yu*) for tea (*cha*)," the water that is the basis of the ceremony itself. The tea pot (*chagama*), made of iron or cast iron, is one of the beautifully handcrafted utensils used in the ceremony, and is intimately connected to the tea-master. They are made by families who have specialized in making tea pots for centuries.

Another word for the tea ceremony is *Sadō*, which translates as the "Way (*dō*) of Tea (*sa*)"; the term therefore emphasizes the aspect of a discipline, of an Art that encompasses all arts.

← *Daruma* doll, used as a good-luck charm by the Japanese Urawa Red Diamonds football team

Sen no Rikyū

The first gatherings with tea were informal, and the drink was served with small plates of food. Over the centuries, these gatherings were formalized by the tea masters who imposed the main principles, and these were transformed into a ceremony. A key figure in this transformation was Sen no Rikyū (1522–1591), a Zen monk and master who trained at the Rinzai Daitokuji Zen temple in Kyoto, to whom we owe the ceremonial form we know today. He became the tea master and personal adviser of the two greatest warlords responsible for the unification of Japan, first Oda Nobunaga (1534–1582), then, upon his death, Toyotomi Hideyoshi (1536–1598). Under the latter, Sen no Rikyū codified the ceremony into a style known as *wabi-cha*, applying the values of sobriety, austerity, poverty, simplicity, and appreciation for imperfection and natural materials, which also dictate the rules of construction and appreciation of artifacts and architectures outside the tea ceremony. This led to the invention of Raku ware and the use of the *kintsugi* technique, the custom of repairing and restoring broken cups and pottery by embellishing the cracks with lacquer and gold.

Following several disagreements, General Hideyoshi ordered Sen no Rikyū to commit *seppuku*, ritual suicide.

↑ The Temple of the Golden Pavilion (*Kinkakuji*) in Kyoto, built by a *shōgun* as a retirement villa in the 14th century, and turned into a temple in the 15th century, during the Muromachi period (1336–1573)

The Golden Pavilion and the Silver Pavilion

There were two *shōguns* who promoted the Zen arts, both of whom built their retirement villas in the hills of Kyoto, making them the main cultural centers of the time.

In 1398, Ashikaga Yoshimitsu built one of the most spectacular buildings in Japan, the Kinkakuji, or Temple of the Golden Pavilion, in the northern hills. The building is completely covered in gold leaf and is reflected on an artificial pond in the center of a large garden reminiscent of the Paradise of Amida Buddha. It was destroyed by arson in 1950, by a mentally ill monk, and only reopened to the public in 1987. It was here that the poetic form *renga* (linked poem) and the *Nō* theater found a

← Black Raku ceramic tea bowl (*chawan*), repaired with lacquer and gold using the traditional *kinstsugi* technique

Zen: Paths of Meditation   47

patron, so much so that Yoshimitsu actually adopted the first great *Nō* theater playwright, Zeami Motokiyo, as a child. In 1489, Ashikaga Yoshimasa, Yoshimitsu's grandson, built the Ginkakuji, or Temple of the Silver Pavilion, in the eastern hills, although it was never actually covered with silver. In the adjacent Togudō Buddha Hall, there is the Dojinsai tearoom, the oldest and smallest in Japan, composed of just four tatamis. Yoshimasa promoted both the tea ceremony and the art of flower arranging, and was the patron of great Zen painters like Tōyō Sesshū.

Chashitsu

In times of war, the tea ceremony was a diplomatic tool; a moment in which the aesthetic appreciation of every detail, from gestures to shapes and materials, became an opportunity for silent dialogue while the weapons were

left outside. The *chashitsu* was performed in small tea rooms, which at the time of Sen no Rikyū were called *sukiya*, and the spaces could be created inside the large aristocratic residences, or in separate huts which could be reached via stone paths that took guests through the beautiful gardens, preparing their spirit for tranquility and contemplation. The elegance of the Shōkintei at Villa Katsura Rikyū, built in Kyoto by Prince Hachijō Toshihito in the early seventeenth century, has influenced all modern Western architects.

Tea and its Utensils

The bushy tea plantations that cover the slopes of the Japanese hills in many regions are some of the most gentle landscapes in the country, and tea is certainly the most sought-after typical local product.

There are many types of green tea, made from the leaves and twigs of the plant, and with different roasting methods and recipes, but Matcha is the most popular for the tea ceremony. It is a dense, bitter tea powder, stored in a caddy (*chaire*), from which the master of the ceremony takes a small amount, using a long bamboo spoon, and puts it into the tea bowl (*chawan*). He then skillfully dissolves it in very little boiling water, by quickly whisking it with a bamboo whisk (*chasen*). It is then offered to the guest and they take three short sips, holding the large cup with both hands, but not before thanking the master, and sweetening their mouth with a piece of candy served specifically for this purpose.

Dry Gardens

There are two *karesansui* (literally "dry mountains and water") Zen gardens that should not go unmentioned. The Daisen-in, a sub-temple of the great Daitoku-ji Temple, completed in 1513 along with the main temple by the monk and landscape architect Kogaku Soko, is based on the Chinese

◀ Interior of a traditional *tatami* room (flooring made of mats measuring 35.5 x 71 in/90 x 180 cm) in the 17th-century villa of the court noble Ichijo Ekan (Ichijo Ekan Sanso), who moved from Kyoto to Kamakura in 1959

model of the Buddhist Treasure Mountain. Thanks to the closely spaced vertical rocks in the background, and the increasingly smaller rocks in front of them, it evokes the image of a mountainous landscape; there is also a stepped waterfall that flows into a stream represented by gravel, from which different-sized stones emerge to symbolize boats, turtles, and fish. A horizontal stone slab crosses the symbolic waterway.

The large Ryōan-ji garden, created by the monk and landscape archi-

▾ View of the "dry garden" (*karesansu*) in the Ryōanji Zen Temple in Kyoto

tect Sōami in around 1520, is completely different. There is a rectangular space, surrounded by a boundary wall on two sides, and a veranda on the other two, which the inner room of the temple overlooks, with islands of rocks in groups of two, three, or five, of different sizes, on an area of raked gravel reminiscent of waves. It is said that at no point can all fifteen stones be seen at the same time, a riddle that is in keeping with a *koan*, an enigma that cannot be solved with logic, but only during meditation.

Theater and Dance: Discipline and Performance

"The subtly enchanting style of a prestigious master of our way, which goes beyond all praise, the feeling that transcends cognition, the visual effect produced by such a style that goes beyond any other style: that is what the flower of beauty will be made of."

— Zeami Motokiyo, On the Art of the Nō Drama

◄ Puppet from the *Bunraku* Theater in Osaka

What do we know about Japanese theater and performing arts? The rhythm of the great *taiko* drums; the lion dance, which we perhaps associate more with Chinese holidays; the masks, without knowing they are only associated with *Nō* theater; the colors and costumes of *kabuki*? This form of theater is still to a certain extent considered strange, feared, linked to the difficulty of linguistic understanding, of translating stories, of the cultural, philosophical, and aesthetic aspects on which Japanese theater is based. Therefore, in the Western imagination, which still knows little or nothing about the tradition of puppet theater, *bunraku* or *jōruri*, there is little difference between the aristocratic, sophisticated *Nō* theater and the popular, colorful *Kabuki* theater.

The fascinating treatise *Fūshikaden (The Transmission of the Flower Through [a Mastery of] the Forms)*, written in 1402 by Zeami Motokiyo, the first playwright to refine the forms of the *Nō* theater, traces the first forms of the *sarugaku* sacred dance, translatable as "monkey dance," back to the legend recounted in the *Kojiki*: the legend has it that the goddess Ama-no-Uzume (or Ame-no-Uzume) performed an improvised dance, accompanied by percussion instruments, dance steps, and singing, in front of the cave in which the Great Sun Goddess Amaterasu had hidden, thereby plunging the world into darkness, arousing the curiosity of the gods, and entertaining them so much that it is believed to be the first Shinto ritual performance.

History

During the Nara period (710–794), dance forms such as *gagaku* were imported from China, later evolving into *bugaku*, and they were performed by professionals in temples, also using small masks. While *sarugaku*, a popular form of entertainment with music, dance, and games, was performed in shrines and during local festivals (*matsuri*), *dengaku* was performed in paddy fields, with professional jugglers and acrobats accompanied by flutes and drums.

The curious thing is that during the Muromachi period (1336–1573), the *Nō* theater came to be defined as *sarugaku-nō*, which was closer to a mimetic drama, and, in the more symbolic form, *dengaku-nō*.

The Nō Theater

Zeami, who had been adopted by the third *shōgun* Ashikaga Yoshimitsu as a child, and who under his patronage was trained for an artistic career with his father Kan'ami in the famous Golden Pavilion in Kyoto, was the first to codify the *nō* theater as we know it today, writing more than two hundred plays. He introduced the concepts of *yūgen* (that is, the grace and elegance that the actor had to embody), and *hana*, (the actor's "flower," referring to the ability to embody the essence of the character they were playing on stage, be it a woman or a man, young or old, a spirit or supernatural being).

The *Nō* theater was originally a product of its time, and therefore not designed to be entertainment, but rather an exercise; based on *kata*, fixed forms the actor practiced daily, one could say that it was similar to a discipline like martial arts. On the other hand, the *Nō* theater arose in an aristocratic environment, in a period marked by great battles between the various military clans; therefore, as well as the tea ceremony and other arts inspired by Zen philosophy, it also perfectly met the need to create moments of silence, calm, and order within disorder, as the codified and simple gestures demonstrate. To lighten the long performances, there was an interval with a *kyogen* performance, a funnier, more comical, and lighter show that today is staged separately. Akira Kurosawa took his inspiration from the *Nō* theater and incorporated it into his 1957 film *The Throne of Blood*.

The Stage

The stage of the *Nō* theater is considered a sacred space, and its extreme simplicity, reminiscent of a small Shinto shrine, is evidence of this. Like the *Sumō* ring, the stage is traditionally covered by a sloping roof, with a sacred rope hung across the top. On the backdrop there is a large evergreen pine tree, potentially where the divine resides, which symbolizes the meeting between the earthly and heavenly worlds, as the plots of the plays recount. White gravel is laid on the ground around the stage, to evoke the ancient outdoor theaters, where it served to reflect sunlight. A side passageway (*hashigakari*) marked by small pine trees leads the actor from the dressing rooms, where they dress and get into character, to the stage.

The Mask

In the *kagami-no-ma* room, or "mirror room," the main actor, the *shite*, puts on a mask, typical only in the *Nō* theater, which represents the character. This is always done ceremoniously, first offering a slight bow of

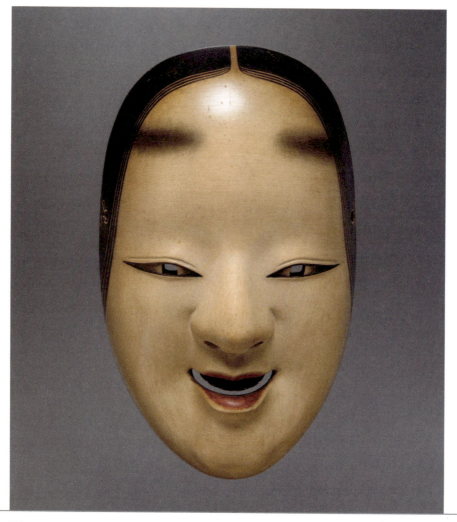

→ Painted wooden mask of a young woman (*ko-omote*), used in *Nō* theater, Edo period (1603–1868)

thanks to the mask in their hands; then, once put on, looking at themselves in the mirror to fully get into character before going on stage. All the props—the mirror, fan, costumes, and mask—are sacred objects (*shintai*), and are a reference to the accessories that the priestesses wore in their sacred dances when imitating the goddess Ama-no-Uzume.

The masks (*nōmen*), carved in wood by specialized artisans and then painted, can represent female and male figures of different ages, demons, or legendary and magical animals such as the fox, the cat, the lion, or figures from the afterlife. The most representative masks are those of a young woman, the *Ko-omote*, which has a sweet, white face, with black hair neatly combed on the sides, and a half-closed red mouth that contrasts with the blackened teeth, and that of a jealous demon, *Hannya*, which epitomizes the transfiguration of female jealousy into a frightening demon with horns, sharp teeth, and terrifying eyes.

← Painted wooden demon mask (*hannya*), used in *Nō* theater, c. 1280

Theater and Dance: Discipline and Performance

Kabuki Theater

Kabuki theater is said to have originated in Kyoto in 1603, from performances by a group of dancers on the banks of the Kamo River, led by Izumo no Okuni. Sadly, in 1629 women were forbidden to perform, and after that the *Kabuki* were performed first by young men, and later, from 1652, by professional male actors who also played the female roles (*onnagata*). The performances are more dramatic, more colorful, and louder than *Nō* theater. There are no masks, but the actors' faces are painted with red, blue, or black bands, depending on the character, emphasizing the facial muscles. *Kabuki* was a new theater that catered to the tastes of the emerging merchant class in the city, which arose following the rapid urbanization of the eastern capital, Edo, today's Tokyo, chosen by the Tokugawa shogunate to be its administrative seat.

Yakushae: Images of Actors

The long period of peace guaranteed by the Tokugawa shogunate resulted in an unparalleled flourishing of the arts, and of the entire world linked to the enjoyment of earthly pleasures; the latter was the favorite subject of the *Ukiyo-e*, the wood-block prints of the floating world, which show how entire neighborhoods dedicated to the theater arose in the city. The streets were full of people and theaters, with banners and billboards announcing the new theatrical season and names of the leading actors, who for the occasion gathered in the street to show their faces to the public (*kaomise*). The image market expanded exponentially, offering views of the theater, both inside and out; of the stage with the best-known plays being performed; of the elation of audiences from all walks of life; but, above all, portraits of the actors on stage, backstage in their dressing rooms, full figures or half busts, stars of the moment who dictated fashion.

→ Utagawa Hiroshige, *Saruwakachō*, from the series *One Hundred Famous Views of Edo*, polychrome wood-block print, 1856 (modern reproduction)

Theater and Dance: Discipline and Performance 59

Trivia

One of the key figures of *Ukiyo-e* was Torii Kiyonobu (1664–1729), founder of the first great school specializing in theater prints, posters (*banzuke*), and portraits of actors, and son of a kabuki theater actor who had moved from Osaka to Edo.

Tōshūsai Sharaku, an artist whose identity has not yet been clarified, introduced the genre of *ōkubi-e*, "large head (or large neck) portraits," which depicted only the head and upper torso of the actors, on beautiful bright backgrounds of mica powder. He only worked for one season, between 1794 and 1795, producing about a hundred and forty prints and then disappearing into thin air, leaving the legend behind him. A series of posters by the greatest twentieth-century graphic designers, including Tanaka Ikkō (1930–2002), was dedicated to him.

One of the most famous and most painted actors of the eighteenth century was the "unparalleled" Ichikawa Danjurō V (1741–1806). He is recognizable by the huge family crest of three nested squares (*mimasu*) on his brick-red robe, his large aquiline nose, and the red lines painted on his face, which is how he appeared in his most important role in the famous play *Shibaraku* ("Wait a minute!"), first staged by Danjurō I in 1697, at the Nakamuraza Theater in Edo.

The Puppet Theater

Throughout the Edo period, the puppet theater, known as *ningyō jōruri* or *bunraku*, competed with the *Kabuki* theater for the audience's attention; they staged the same plays, often written for one style of theater and then adapted for the other. One of the great playwrights who deserves a mention is Chikamatsu Monzaemon (1653–1724), from Kyoto, who wrote for both theaters, leading to the *jōruri* being successful up until the first half of the eighteenth century, with historical stories of

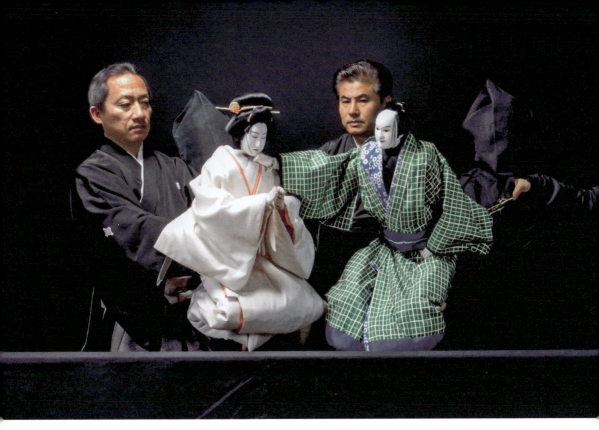

▲ A puppet theater show (*bunraku*) in Osaka, staged by puppet master Kiritake Kanjurō (left), designated a "Living National Treasure"

warriors and nobles, but also of current events.

Of the latter genre, the plot of *Sonezaki Shinjū* ("The Love Suicides at Sonezaki") is famous, and was evoked in Takeshi Kitano's beautiful film *Dolls*, 2002, in which the protagonists drag a red rope that ties them together, a symbol of destiny keeping them indissolubly bound together.

Another modern reinterpretation was proposed under the artistic direction of the famous photographer and artist Hiroshi Sugimoto, in his show *Sugimoto bunraku. Sonezaki Shinjū*, which toured Europe in 2013.

The large puppets are moved by puppeteers, today recognized as Living National Treasures, who often create and dress them according to their own tastes, just as tea masters do with their tea bowls. Today's most well-known theater is the National Bunraku Theater in Osaka, with puppeteer Kanjurō Kiritake.

Eating with the Eyes

In the cuisine of any country, efforts no doubt are made to have the food harmonize with the tableware and the walls; but with Japanese food, a brightly lighted room and shining tableware cut the appetite in half.

— *Tanizaki Jun'ichirō*, In Praise of Shadows
  (Original title: *In'ei raisan, 1933*)

← 24-hour Ramen vending machine (*jidōhanbaiki*), making eating possible at any time of the day or night

From ramen to sushi, sake, and matcha green tea, Japanese cuisine, or Washoku, has become part of culinary fashions and everyday life, no longer just reserved for special occasions and a few cultured diners, but widely available as affordable and trendy street food. In 2013, Washoku was also recognized as a UNESCO Intangible Cultural Heritage of Humanity.

The expression *kaiseki ryōri* defines the most sophisticated cuisine, made up of countless small delicacies served in an infinity of plates and glasses, bowls and baskets, in different shapes, sizes, colors, and materials: one's appetite is whetted just by looking at the ceramic, lacquer, wicker, and cast-iron tableware covered with food, placed almost randomly in front of the diner, combining all the colors of the seasons. This is also a Chinese custom, from which Japan has inherited the foundations of its cuisine, and which it highly respects; Chinese and non-Japanese restaurants are, in fact, often chosen for important official dinners.

Kaiseki cuisine derives from the small portions of food that were served during gatherings where tea was served, which later became the tea ceremony. Today it is offered by the most renowned and sought-after restaurants, where, in addition to very fresh ingredients, you can also enjoy an extremely elegant atmosphere and the simplicity of the furnishings, in intimate rooms surrounded by movable walls and soft lights, enhancing the aromas and colors of the dishes.

The dishes are decorated with seasonal leaves, flower petals, shoots, fruits, and berries, either real or made of edible ingredients.

The Five Elements

Japanese cuisine is said to be based on five philosophical principles which correspond to the five elements of nature. Earth, water, fire, metal, and air "create" five flavors (*gomi*: sweet, sour, salty, bitter and umami), five senses (*gokan*), five colors (*goshiki*), and five techniques (*goho*). Japanese tableware always comes in sets of five, and they prefer asymmetry, irregular shapes, and diverse colors to the typical homogeneity of Western tableware. Not only are the colors of the food balanced by how they are arranged in the bowl, plate, or glass, but the color of the dishes is also chosen carefully to evoke a feeling: green/blue (*ao*) to promote relaxation; yellow (*ki*) and red (*aka*) to stimulate the appetite; white (*shiro*) to evoke a sense of cleanliness; black (*kuro*) and tea brown (*cha*) at the end of the meal.

Suggested Reading

↘ Dōgen – Kosho Uchiyama Roshi, **How to Cook Your Life. From the Zen Kitchen to Enlightenment**, published by Shambhala, 2005

↓ A selection of vegan dishes from the Zen temple cuisine (*shojin ryōri*) at the Taizoin Temple in Kyoto

Shojin ryōri, the Buddhist Cuisine

Today, vegetarian or vegan cuisine, eaten and made by Buddhist monks in the monasteries, is also highly appreciated by foreign visitors due to its healthfulness, and is a tradition from which the principles of *kaiseki* also originate. These meals are also served as small portions of different dishes, but without meat, fish, or ingredients of animal origin, reducing the condiments to a bare minimum, and enhancing only the taste of the raw materials, which are obviously seasonal. You can try this cuisine in the temples' guesthouses, which are also open to visitors, combining meditation and morning prayer with a breakfast prepared by the monks; but there are also several restaurants that have specialized in this type of cuisine, creating extremely sophisticated dishes.

When examining the rice, first check for sand; when examining the sand [sifted from the rice], first check for rice. [...] When steaming rice, treat the pot as one's own head; when rinsing the rice, know that the water is one's own lifeblood. Keep a sharp eye on everything, so as not to waste even a single grain, and properly rinse out any foreign objects. (p. 18)

Tenzo kyōkun, or *Instructions for a Zen Cook*, is a short essay written in the 13th century, in the Kamakura period, by Dōgen Kigen Zenji (1200–1253), the greatest Zen master and monk. It is the first chapter of his book *Pure Standards for the Zen Community (Eihei Shingi)*, in which he sets out the guidelines and spirit of daily monastic life through teachings, parables, and Zen riddles (*kōan*) to stimulate meditation. Dōgen believed rice was the basic element of daily Zen practices, and that of all those who carried out daily work, the monastery cook (the *tenzo*) was most symbolic of the meditative discipline Zazen. The *tenzo* is neither a cook nor a servant; he was one of the six office-holders who guided the monastic community. Washing and preparing rice and vegetables for breakfast, making lunch and dinner for the monks, washing the dishes, putting the pots and utensils away neatly, and making sure there

→ Some souvenirs at the Fushimi Inari Taisha Shrine in Kyoto, famous for its endless row of red *torii* gates dedicated to Inari, the Shinto deity of rice cultivation

↳ *Kome*, Rice

Rice accompanies Japanese meals and is the basis for flours, desserts, sake, and sushi. In the Japanese language, the term for rice is commonly accompanied by the honorific prefix "o": *okome*, "honorable rice"; and if this is not enough for you to understand just how much the subsistence of the Japanese people has been linked to this food for centuries, you should know that the term *gohan*, which is the word for meal (*han*) with the honorific prefix "go," and can be translated as "honorable meal," essentially refers to a bowl of white rice.

In pictorial tradition, there are hilarious parodies that show battle scenes between rivals made of rice: sake and *mochi*, soft, sweet sticky cakes in the shape of a ball, usually served on a skewer.

Eating with the Eyes

▴ A typical fast-food restaurant in Sapporo serving sushi on a conveyor belt (*kaitenzushi*)

are enough ingredients for the next day, are not jobs to delegate to subordinates, but rather "a practice that requires exerting all your energies," using your own hands.

Animals and Robots at the Table

Let's dispel the myth of sushi being an everyday food. Tasting fresh sushi and sashimi, while sitting at the counter watching a specialized chef fillet the fish with very sharp knives, peel the vegetables, grate the wasabi, and magically roll the *neta* (the rice base on which the fish is placed) in the palm of their hand, is one of the most sensory and intimate experiences you will have. On the other hand, the post-war resurgence also led to this delicacy being popularized, and in 1958 the first restaurant opened in Osaka, where sushi was served ready-made on plates on a conveyor belt, from which customers helped themselves from the tables on each side. This type of automated restaurant is called *Kaitenzushi*, and it is still very popular, and people go to them for quick, cheap snacks at all times of the day.

You can also enjoy hot and cold ramen and soba soups, and small tempura vegetables at tiny stores in the corners of stations, in the subways, and along the streets; you order what you want from the automatic machines at the entrance of the store and get a coupon to collect your ready-made dish from the kitchen. The vending machines (*Jidōhanbaiki*, commonly abbreviated to *hanbaiki* or *jihanki*), which until a few years ago distributed mostly drinks and snacks, now also distribute—non-stop—ready-to-go food from renowned stores.

Technology has taken over in some places, with the waiters replaced by robots, even in *Shabu Shabu* restaurants, one of the most elegant types of restaurants, which specialize in very thinly sliced meat boiled lightly in a pot of steaming broth, which is placed in the center of the table. They are mostly simple robots that bring food from the kitchen

Trivia

- *Itadakimasu* means "enjoy your meal." Everyone at the table says it together before starting a meal, while making a slight bow or placing their hands together as a sign of humble gratitude for receiving the food on the table.
- *Bentobako*: a traditional box for carrying a packed lunch, either stackable or compartmentalized.
- *Teishoku*: a set menu in restaurants, usually offered at a lower price at lunchtime; it is served on a tray and includes a main dish, a hot *miso* soup, a small portion of *tsukemono* (pickled vegetables), and a bowl of boiled white rice.
- *Onigiri*: Japan's most popular snack made of steamed rice, shaped into a ball or a triangle and wrapped in a sheet of dried nori seaweed; they can also be filled with a pinch of *umeboshi* plum, fish, or *konbu* seaweed.
- *Kappamaki*: a type of *maki*, a sushi-roll in the form of a cigar, consisting of rice wrapped in a sheet of dried *nori* seaweed, filled with cucumber instead of raw fish (*makizushi*). It is named after the *kappa*, a mythological creature that loves cucumbers.

- **Kappabashi**: a street in the Asakusa area of Tokyo, where you can spend hours looking at display cabinets filled with *sanpuru* (from the English "sample"), which are plastic models of all types of food, the same that restaurants display in their windows to make choosing from the menu easier. Some stores offer the possibility of participating in a workshop where they are made.
- **Yakatabune**: typical river boats adorned with lanterns, where you can enjoy a trip on a summers evening while dining with friends or loved ones; you can see them in Tokyo Bay, for example.
- **Yatai**: traditional street stalls, in the past run by nearby restaurants, where you can enjoy a quick dish of sushi and other small snacks.

to the tables, some of which have tablets and digital displays to help them communicate with customers. One of the most fascinating is BellaBot, a cat-shaped robot with a tablet that displays feline facial expressions, which uses cat "slang" when talking. An alternate and increasingly fashionable universe is *Animal Cafes*, places where you can interact with all kinds of baby animals, which roam free among the customers: cats, dogs, but also otters, hedgehogs, capybaras, and guinea pigs.

Wagashi

These Japanese sweets are the most beautiful things to eat with your eyes, and their sweetness and texture is far removed from anything found in the West. From colorful flower or leaf-shaped candy, served before matcha green tea during a tea ceremony to counteract the bitterness, to sweets evoking the shapes and colors of nature, created with wooden molds or by hand, made of cane sugar, red bean paste (*anko*), and rice flour, and jellies (*yokan*), either plain or transparent with shapes inside, as if they were aquariums. These confections mark the changes in nature,

← *Yokan* jelly candy made of red *azuki* bean paste, agar, and brown sugar

↑ The iconic cat from the animated film *Doraemon*, on a plate of the traditional *dorayaki* cookies made of red azuki bean paste, his favorite snack

so much so that historical brands only offer specific forms of sweets on certain days of the year, following designs handed down in precious sample books for centuries. Around the shrines and temples, there are colorful stalls selling bananas, apples, and strawberries dipped in chocolate, sweet rice dumplings on a skewer (*dango*), soft fish-shaped cookies that bring you good luck (*taiyaki*), or disc-shaped biscuits (*dorayaki*) filled with anko red bean paste, which have become famous because they are the robot cat Doraemon's favorite food.

↓ Before entering the Meiji Jingu Shrine, visitors and pilgrims must perform a purification ritual using water poured from a long bamboo ladle

Eating with the Eyes

Eating with the Eyes

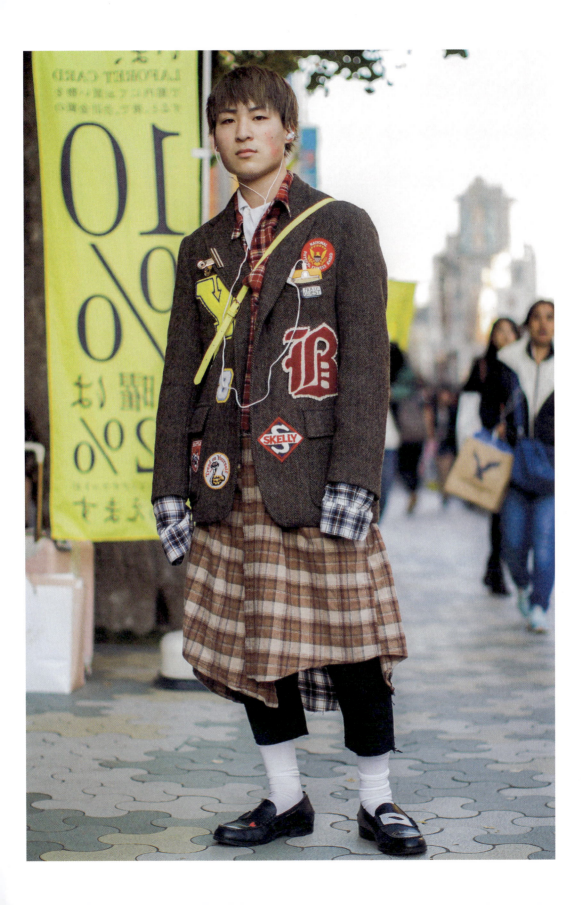

Not Just Kimonos: From Fashion Streets to Catwalks

"The Empress and the other ladies were dressed in the most splendid costumes made of glossy, plum-blossom material, some with heavily figured designs, others decorated with embroidery. On top they wore Chinese jackets of light green, willow green, or red plum-blossom."

— Sei Shōnagon, The Pillow Book, 10th century

◀ Two teenagers in the Harajuku area of Tokyo, famous for its vintage and street fashion stores

Alongside the traditional image of Japan that is associated with the kimono, as if it were a unique and immutable garment, there is now also a strong and varied idea of contemporary Japanese fashion. On the one hand, this is linked to the great twentieth-centurydesigners who experimented and successfully introduced to the catwalk a conception of the body that was different from that proposed by the West, and, on the other, to the spontaneity of street fashion, which offered interesting ideas for the creation of new, more popular and widespread brands.

The word "kimono" is composed of two Chinese characters, and simply means a "thing to wear." Although it is commonly thought of as a robe with long, rectangular sleeves, made of painted or embroidered silk, which wraps around the body to give it a tubular shape and is tied tightly at the waist with a wide, stiff sash, it has to be said that this is a reductive view of a complex world that is continuously evolving: one that involves shapes, colors, fabrics, and accessories dictated by written or unspoken rules that have been shared for centuries.

If you go to buy fabric at a store specializing in kimonos, you will find that it is sold in long rolls, the height of which corresponds to narrow rectangles, which when sewn together without being shaped form the front and back of the kimono, the two square sleeves, and the lapel. The length of a kimono is standard, adjusted while the person is wearing it by making a fold and securing it with thin cords tied around the waist, which are then covered by the *obi*, the wide, stiff sash that embellishes the garment with colors, decorative motifs, and intricate knots at the back. In the Edo period, as can be seen in many paintings, only the courtesans who worked in the pleasure districts wore the long *obi* loosely knotted at the front, a distinctive feature used to make their profession known. A kimono's quality and use is still conveyed by simple bows or more intricate knots today, as well as by other details.

A Kimono for Every Occasion

Yes, because kimonos are not all the same. The short-sleeved *kosode* is the most common one, worn by adult women on all types of for-

▲ Two *obi* knots tied at the back of two women to secure their kimonos

mal occasions. The kimono with the long swinging sleeves is the *furisode*, and is for girls and young unmarried women; it has bright colors and bright floral motifs, and is worn for the *Seijin no hi*, the January ceremony that marks one's entry into adulthood, when the girls pose in photographic studios for their official portrait. The *yukata* is a cotton summer kimono, also often given to guests as a gown at traditional *ryōkan* inns, but above all ideal for hot summer evenings, when you can enjoy a walk with a fan in your hand, and in crowded streets during popular festivals. Today, tourists from around the world can rent a *yukata*, and there are specific campaigns encouraging people to wear them on the streets of Kyoto. The *haori*, on the other hand, is a short jacket for men and women, made of very lightweight gauze or painted silk, with traditional landscapes and subjects on the inner lining; the back and sleeves can also display the family crest (*kamon*). Another garment that is worn over a kimono is the *uchikake*, which is even more precious than the kimono itself, often made of silk brocade or embroidered all over with gold and silver threads; they are not worn with an *obi* around the waist, but left open, allowing the heavy padded hems to form a train behind the wearer.

In the Edo period, the great courtesans who walked along the streets of the pleasure districts from inn to inn attracted customers and visitors precisely by swaying the train behind them, while the garment stood slightly out from the neck, revealing the very seductive "V" shape of white make-up on their pink skin. You can still be seduced by geisha today, as they walk quickly through the streets of Kyoto's Gion district in the evening, although the *uchikake* is only worn for important ceremonies and festivities. The costumes worn by dancers and Shinto priests in *nō* and *kyōgen* theater are called *shōzoku*, a term that actually refers to formal garments derived from the short jackets.

The quality of each type of kimono is variable, depending on the fabric and weaving, from brocade to silk crepe made of natural fibers such as cotton, banana, hemp, and ramie, and the dyeing and decoration technique, from hand-painting to printing with resist techniques, using stencil or rice starch paste, and resist dyeing techniques like *shibori*—all of which contribute to defining a kimono's function.

Ceremonies

In the Shinto wedding ceremony, the bride wears a pure white *shiromuku* kimono that has a large hood; the groom wears the traditional *hakama*, skirt-like pants with wide pleats, similar to those used in martial arts, and a *haori* jacket.

Girls and boys are also made to wear *furisode* and *hakama*, respectively, for the Shichi-Go-San festival, a ceremony that takes place in November, when girls and boys aged three, boys aged five, and girls aged seven go to a shrine to pray for their good health and well-being.

→ A girl with a paper umbrella (*wagasa*) and floral decorations in her hair

Books, Theatre, Music

- *Yukio Mishima*, Forbidden Colors, Vintage Books, 1999 (The novel *Kinjiki*, published between 1951 and 1953, uses the term in the sense of homosexual eroticism, and it is therefore prohibited. This gave rise to *Kinjiki*, the debut performance of Hijikata Tatsumi, founder of butō dance theater, staged at Dai-Ichi Seimei Hall in 1959. It was also the inspiration for Ryūichi Sakamoto's song *Forbidden Colors*, with the lyrics by David Sylvian, included on the album *Merry Christmas, Mr. Lawrence*, MCA Records, 1983.)

- **Kuki Shūzō**, *The Structure of Iki*, translated by John Clark, Power Publications, Sydney, 2011. (A paper explaining what was considered seductive and vulgar, from love to fashion and art, in the early decades of the nineteenth century.)

- **Sei Shōnagon**, *The Pillow Book*, Penguin Classics, 2007 (The brief notes and reflections of a Japanese writer and court lady tell us what was and what was not liked and considered fashionable in a court during the Heian period.)

Dressing According to Etiquette

During the classical Heian period (794–1185), as in the previous Nara period, there was a dress code called *kasane no irome*, which dictated the layered color combinations for the clothes of men, women, and children, depending on the rank they held within the court and imperial family and varying according to holidays and seasons. The women of the court wore up to twelve layers of different-colored robes (*jūnihitoe*) to obtain new colors or shades through transparency, which, like a perfume, evoked nature, leaving a glimpse of the staggered edges of the sleeves, collar, and lower train of the different layered kimonos. There were obviously also forbidden colors (*kinjiki*) for ordinary people, because they were reserved for members of the imperial family; these were the ones obtained from the most expensive dyes, such as gold yellow or *murasaki* purple.

In the Edo period (1603–1868), everything that was considered fashionable was defined with the term *iki*, which means not only the ability to wear and carry accessories with class, but also the ability to seduce without showing off. The Tokugawa military government

→ A woman being dressed in the ancient formal court dress consisting of twelve-layers (*jūnihitoe*)

Not Just Kimonos: From Fashion Streets to Catwalks

repeatedly issued edicts to curb the luxury sought after by the enriched merchant class, and—perhaps alongside the diffusion of a sober elegance that arose around the tea ceremony—they developed a taste for subdued colors like brown and shades of blue and gray, decorated with small motifs and thin vertical stripes; the red or richly painted inner linings could only be admired in private, while in public they could be glimpsed on the sleeves or hem.

From Kimonos to Catwalks

Today, Moriguchi Kunihiko's kimonos are considered works of art, and he has earned the title of "Living National Treasure" thanks to his mastery in the traditional *yūzen* resist dyeing technique, applied to innovative geometric motifs, with optical illusions that are still inspired by natural elements such as flowers, steam, water, and snow. It was, however, Takanashi Hiroko who rejuvenated the kimono, making it popular through a fusion of art and fashion: her works are exhibited in the Victoria & Albert Museum and Japan House London.

The kimono has inspired generations of Japanese designers, from Kenzō Takada to Hanae Mori, Issey Miyake, and Yohji Yamamoto, right up to Rei Kawakubo and his brand Comme des Garçons, and Junko Koshino and Reiko Sudō, who started making their way on European catwalks in the 1960s, upending the concept of Western corporeality and wearability. Mori opened her atelier in 1951, and her works include costumes for *Madame Butterfly* at La Scala opera house in 1985, and Nureyev's *Cinderella* at the Paris Opera in 1986. Yamamoto, one of her contemporaries, went from wrapping the body in a tubular kimono to creating androgynous and covertly seductive torn, deconstructed shapes, which play with monochromatic colors and shadows created by layers of fabric. Miyake, on the other hand, was an innovator, creating sculptural, pleated, three-dimensional, and geometric clothes, but also garments made from

↑ Installations similar to samurai armor created by designer Issey Miyake, exhibited at the National Art Centre in Tokyo in 2016

just one piece of cloth, in which fashion, craftsmanship, art, and technological research become inseparable, as evidenced by his collaborations with the architect Tadao Andō, designers Ikko Tanaka and Tadanori Yokoo, photographers Yasumasa Morimura and Nobuyoshi Araki, and a team of engineers.

Kawakubo was able to subvert the traditional concept of female

beauty by presenting oversized garments, using black, and deconstructing the conventions of symmetry and the idea of the "correct" position for sleeves, cuffs, and seams. Koshino's opera and theater costumes are futuristic, utopian sculptures, a combination of shape and carefully selected materials. The textile designer Sudō is moving in a different direction with her brand NUNO, now well-known throughout the world, also in museums, for her experimental and innovative textiles based on her studies and research on traditional local techniques.

Fashion Areas

Omotesandō, the long tree-lined shopping street in the heart of Tokyo that connects the amazing Kengo Kuma Nezu Museum to the Meiji Shrine and Harajuku district, is home to the most beautiful stores and showrooms of various lines by the stylists Miyake and Yamamoto, as well as the historic Hanae Mori Building.

Harajuku, the heart of street fashion, a rockabilly district in the 1970s, and a meeting point for young Lolitas, Gothic girls, and street musicians until the early 2000s; you can still soak up this atmosphere on Takeshita Dōri and the adjoining streets, which are overflowing with vintage and second-hand stores, and cosplay costume stores, ranging from punk-dark to the sweet and childish *kawaii*.

Roppongi, behind Tokyo Midtown; the 21_21 Design Sight museum, founded by Issey Miyake and designed by Tadao Ando, is nestled amongst the greenery of a large park, and is the venue for design, art, architecture, fashion, and engineering exhibitions that test the boundaries between different fields of research. It is an origami-like low-rise structure, inspired by Miyake's "A Piece of Cloth" concept.

Roppongi, Axis Design Center, a building dedicated to design, whose basement houses the beautiful NUNO store, a must-see for its beautiful fabrics.

← Two girls on the streets of Tokyo dressed as vintage dolls, following the Dolly-kei fashion style

Protagonists and Places of Contemporary Art

"Polka dots can't stay alone. When we obliterate nature and our bodies with polka dots, we become part of the unity of our environments."
—*Yayoi Kusama*

← Interior view of the National Art Center Tokyo (NACT). It is situated in the Roppongi district, and was designed by Kisho Kurokawa

There are all kinds of galleries, foundations, and museums scattered throughout Japan: public but also private, linked to temples, shrines, universities, and historic companies and foundations, which over time have built large collections of art, mostly at the beginning of the twentieth century, or during the economic boom of the 1980s and 1990s. Many places are known for their collections, others are completely unknown and sometimes mysterious in their contents, while yet others are selected tourist destinations because they were designed by famous architects or built in places of great natural beauty.

The national museums of Tokyo, Kyoto, Nara, and Kyushu are part of the state museum network that preserves most of the Japanese collections and treasures, with paintings, sculptures, and art ranging from prehistory to modern times. Then there are those dedicated to modern and contemporary art, such as the National Museum of Modern Art, Tokyo (MOMAT), close to the Imperial Palace; the Kyoto Museum (MOMAK), near the Grand Heian Shrine; and the National Art Center, Tokyo (NACT), situated in the heart of Roppongi: the building, designed by Kisho Kurokawa, a well-known exponent of the Metabolism movement, is made entirely of glass, steel, and concrete, and has large undulating walls. And all this is not to mention the National Museum of Western Art in Ueno Park in Tokyo, designed by Le Corbusier, which is considered a UNESCO heritage site; the National Museum of International Art in Osaka; and the Ishikawa National Museum of Applied Arts in Kanazawa.

Contemporary Places

In the late nineties, Tokyo's Roppongi district, previously considered peripheral and unsafe, underwent massive urban transformation, thanks to the construction of multi-functional skyscrapers and prestigious buildings designed by important architects to house contemporary art and design museums.

The first building to advance change was the Mori group's monumental skyscraper, a tubular glass tower called Roppongi Hills Mori Tower, designed by Richard Gluckman and completed in 2003. It has 54 floors and is 781 feet (238 meters) high, and the Observation Deck offers a breathtaking 360° view of the metropolis. The tower defined an urban development model known as the "vertical

↑ The "21_21 Design Sight" in Roppongi Midtown, Tokyo, founded by Issey Miyake and designed by architect Tadao Ando

city-garden" concept, which then inspired ARK Hills, Toranomon Hills, and the recent Azabudai Hills Mori JP Tower, all in Roppongi.

The 33-foot-high (10 meters) spider-shaped sculpture by French sculptor Louise Bourgeois stands in the elevated square in front of the Mori Tower, while the fifty-second and fifty-third floors house the Mori Art Museum, renowned for its contemporary art exhibitions by world-famous artists such as Ai Weiwei, Yayoi Kusama, Takashi Murakami, and Aida Makoto.

The Suntory Museum is just a short walk away, in Roppongi Midtown, another cultural area, although more recent. Nearby, there is also the National Art Centre, Tokyo, a multi-functional space built in 2007 and designed to hold temporary exhibitions rather than permanent collections (this is where the two most important Kusama Yayoi and Issey Miyake exhibitions were held), and the 21_21 Design Sight, a concrete building designed for Issey Miyake by Tadao Ando in 2007. Its origami-like architecture was inspired by Miyake's APOC—or "A Piece of Cloth"—apparel concept. The building hosts exhibition projects based on a wide range of experimental and interdisciplinary themes regarding design, fashion, engineering, architecture, graphics, art, and crafts, making it unique in the Japanese landscape. The new Artizon Museum, formerly the Bridgestone Museum that relocated to a newly built building in Kyobashi, moves away from the nucleus of original European and Japanese modern art to focus on contemporary design, with a new mission which—as its name suggests—looks to the future.

The Great Masters of Contemporary Art

Not many contemporary Japanese artists have gained international recognition; but of those who have, **Yayoi Kusama**—now well-known to the general public, thanks to her collaboration with the Louis Vuitton brand—is worthy of note. During the campaign, the artist's installations were exhibited everywhere: her polka-dotted pumpkins were on display in the windows and squares of the world's most important cities, and there was a gigantic sculpture of her painting the brand's building in Paris with her brush. However, she has had a very long career, one that has also been marked by dejection. When she moved to the United States in the 1950s—she held her first exhibition in Seattle in 1957—she was faced with the movements of the time and celebrities like Andy Warhol. It was a difficult period, and this also led her to think about committing suicide. We can see just how much art is linked to Kusama's psycholog-

→ Art installation by Kusama Yayoi, on the island of Naoshima ical condition, and how it is the only therapy and way for her to exist, in her obsessive repetitiveness of objects or spaces covered entirely with clusters of padded phallic forms made out of cloth; in the paintings and installations entirely obliterated with polka dots, the huge pumpkins being the form best known to the public; and in the Infinity Mirror Rooms, rooms filled with mirrors and spheres creating endless reflections, which she herself entered and lost herself in, camouflaging herself in the work. She returned to Japan in 1975, and has lived, by choice, in the Seiwa psychiatric hospital since 1977, which she leaves almost every morning to go to her atelier.

As well as being part of the collections in many museums around the world, her works are permanently visible in Japan, at the museum in Matsumoto, her hometown, and in the spaces of the Benesse Foundation at the Valley Gallery, on Naoshima; this is where the installation *Narcissus Garden* is, while her *Yellow Pumpkin*, restored after being swept up by a typhoon on August 9, 2021, is on a small pier on the same island.

Protagonists and Places of Contemporary Art

Takashi Murakami, an artist known for his sculptures of giant mushrooms and smiling daisies, as well as for Mr. Dob, his alter ego created in 1993, was chosen for the 2003 Louis Vuitton campaign. He has exhibited in major international museums, at the Venice Biennale in 2003, and at the Palace of Versailles in 2010. Promoter and major exponent of the Superflat pop art movement inspired by manga and anime, his artist collective Kaikai Kiki, founded as the Hiropon Factory in 1995 and then developed in its Tokyo and New York headquarters, created industrial collective art production.

↓ Yoshitomo Nara, *In the Pink Lake* (2004), exhibited at
The World According to Nara exhibition at One Pacific Place in Admiralty, Hong Kong

Another ironic pop artist who is influenced by traditional Japanese art and inspired by manga and anime, is **Nara Yoshitomo**, a cartoonist and illustrator known for his portraits of dogs and girls with grim, menacing expressions which denounce society's corruption of childhood innocence. His Ukiyo-e series is also famous; there, he uses the icons of the masters of the Floating World, such as Hokusai, Hiroshige, and Utamaro, inserting figures of angry girls and aggressive dogs, along with graffiti to create social commentary.

↓ Yoshitomo Nara, *Round Eyes* (2009), exhibited at *The World According to Nara* exhibition at One Pacific Place in Admiralty, Hong Kong

Protagonists and Places of Contemporary Art

The Great Master of Photography

Japan is the place for photography and high-tech camera technology. Everyone remembers the groups of tourists who traveled the world in the '80s and '90s, with a camera around their neck, ready to take a photo. Japan's late nineteenth-century hand-colored photographs, using watercolors and aniline dyes, are also highly appreciated. They were sold as souvenirs to the first foreigners who arrived in the archipelago, and collected, mostly abroad. Another Japanese phenomenon is the tiny photographs (*purikura*) taken inside the photo booths (*Purint Club machines*) dotted around public spaces, which can be customized manually by adding writing and stickers. This boom was popular with teenagers in the 1990s; but although there are still booths around today, they are obviously not as popular, due to mobile phones and emojis. The widespread dissemination of photography also gave rise to the *Onnanoko Shashinka* movement, a group of young female artists who made their private and everyday lives a new subject in photos presented in the form of a photo diary. This is a new, intimate, and feminine photographic genre, today represented by professionals such as Hiromix, Mika Ninagawa, Yurie Nagashima, Tomoko Sawada, Miwa Yanagi, and Mari Katayama.

Among the exponents of official photography, we cannot overlook Daido Moriyama and his street photography, or Nobuyoshi Araki, known, above all, for his erotic and at the same time ironic portraits of Japanese women presented in forms of physical bondage, with toy dinosaurs next to bodies semi-clothed in kimonos. Another important exponent is Hiroshi Sugimoto, with his crystalline black and white photos of the ocean and the central horizon line, or those of forked lightning hitting the ground, but also the series on the dioramas of natural-history museums and wax museums, where the boundaries between truth and illusion are blurred. Yasumasa Morimura is also good at playing with these boundaries, which he does very provocatively, disguising and transforming himself into historical figures such as Einstein, Hitler, and Mao, but also Frida and Marilyn Monroe, while maintaining his own oriental features.

→ Japanese photographer Nobuyoshi Araki in Paris

↳ **Setouchi Triennale**

The Setouchi Triennale is one of the most popular contemporary art events. It is held on the islands of Naoshima, Teshima, Megijima, Ogijima, Shodoshima, Oshima, Inujima, Shamijima, Honjima, Takamishima, Awashima, and Ibukijima, with permanent installations and temporary exhibitions by internationally renowned artists scattered throughout the spaces, both indoors and outdoors. But it is also a land-reclamation project, as some of these small islands in the Seto Inland Sea were once only used for dumping waste. The fulcrum of the project is the Benesse Art Site on Naoshima, developed by the foundation of the same name, which includes the beautiful Chichu Art Museum, designed by Tadao Ando and built in 2004 under a hill, but also a luxurious hotel, installations by Hiroshi Sugimoto, including his Glass Tea Room and the **Go'o Shrine**, the Lee Ufan Museum designed by Tadao Ando, and a public bath house (sentō), the Naoshima Bath, renovated by Shinro Otake for the entire population. On the island of Teshima, there is the Teshima Art Museum built by Rei Naito and architect Ryue Nishizawa, as well as Teshima Yokoo House, dedicated to the graphic designer and artist Tadanori Yokoo. In the woods in the middle of a lake, there is the Tom Na H-iu installation by Mariko Mori, inspired by Celtic rites.

↑ Tadanori Yokoo, the dry garden at *Teshima Yokoo House*, a permanent work on the island of Teshima, part of the Setouchi Triennale since 2013
→ Kenji Yanobe, *The Star Anger* installation at the port of Sakate on the island of Shodo, part of the Setouchi Triennale since 2013

Japan As It Appears in Literature and Films

"I have always said that I only make tofu because I am a tofu maker. One person cannot make so many different kinds of films. It is possible to eat many different types from around the world at a restaurant in a Japanese department store; but as a result of this overly abundant selection, the quality of the food and its taste suffers. Filmmaking is the same way. Even if my films appear to all be the same, I am always trying to express something new, and I have a new interest in each film. I am like a painter who keeps painting the same rose over and over again."

— *Yasujirō Ozu*

While the eighties and nineties were marked by an image created by the great Japanese filmography of directors such as Nagisa Oshima, Hiroshi Teshigahara, Akira Kurosawa, and Yasujirō Ozu, followed by auteurs like Takeshi Kitano and Hirokazu Kore-eda, the last few decades have also seen increasingly more Japanese literature being translated into Western languages: works by Banana Yoshimoto and Murakami Haruki, for example, but also by great twentieth-century authors such as Yukio Mishima, Jun'ichirō Tanizaki, and Yasunari Kawabata.

← A portrait of the Japanese actor, comedian, and director Takeshi Kitano

One of the qualities of Japanese literature and cinema is undeniably the ability to pay attention to and recount the small events in everyday life: events that would undoubtedly fall into oblivion in the great sagas and epic stories where heroic action counts, because they are trivial and part of that everyday routine that is not worth the recording.

Starting from the personal diaries (*nikki*) and collections of the thoughts and random notes of court ladies in the Heian period (794–1185), written in Japanese—such as *Murasaki Shikibu nikki* (*The Diary of Lady Murasaki*) or *Makura no sōshi* (*The Pillow Book*) by Sei Shōnagon—we can see the meticulous descriptions of details: of the slow passing of time; of significant, yet almost frivolous, feelings; in some way giving dignity to aspects that would otherwise just be in the background, thereby bringing them to the forefront: the appropriateness of clothing/accessory combinations; preparations for going to the temple; seasonal changes in the garden; and so forth.

Banana Yoshimoto

Attention to detail is something that is also found in the works of Banana Yoshimoto, a well-known author of contemporary women's literature. She conquered the Western public with the simplicity of her descriptions of small, humble things, and of the most intimate and universal feelings, yet at the same time revealing the most profound problems in Japanese society today. Banana Yoshimoto has captured Western audiences by opening doors to a lot of Japanese literature, while also attracting critics

▶ Katsushika Hokusai, *Young Woman Reading "The Pillow Book (makura no soshi),"* polychrome wood-block print, Surimono, 1822

Japan As It Appears in Literature and Films

who accused her of being superficial. Her first book *Kitchin (Kitchen)*, released in 1988, immediately became a world best seller, providing a new literary model that seemed to be reminiscent of the essentiality of manga; the following year it was made into a film by director Yoshimitsu Morita, just as happened to her book *Tsugumi* (1989), which was made into a film by Jun Ishikawa.

Yasujirō Ozu

If we look at great Japanese cinema, it was the work of the director Ozu (1903–1963)—who made over fifty movies in his long career—that uniquely and extremely intimately transposed stories about life, human feelings and relationships, and atmospheres of lived-in places full of nostalgia. He did this through his signature style, which involved slow sequences, static shots, and frames showing scenes involving more people, more characters. Ozu, who began his career with silent movies, was able to tell the story by leaving its structure to silence and pauses; his movies are, in fact, a good representation of the essentiality of the Japanese language, in which the unspoken and the unshown counts more and is more emotionally charged than what is made explicit. This also applies to monochrome ink paintings, in which the spaces left blank, or filled with fog, mist, or clouds painted in grayish ink diluted with a little water, then sprinkled with gold dust, dictate the atmosphere of the entire painted landscape. It is the same in Shinto temples, where the presence of the divine is hidden inside inaccessible buildings, and in design and dry gardens, where the landscape is created by removing and excluding elements.

Just as the plates and bowls are arranged in front of diners on a Japanese table, so they can choose which one to pick from, Ozu's camera arranges the sequences of his movies in front of the observer in an equal, linear, and

← The writer Mahoko Yoshimoto, aka Banana Yoshimoto

natural way, with no hierarchy, using frontal shots. Ozu wanted "to make people feel what life is like without delineating all the dramatic ups and downs," avoiding excess but making people feel indirectly the big events in the story. His masterpieces, which are symbols of Japanese realism, are about Japanese society, living traditions, and the consequences of post-war modernity and Westernization, the family and its dynamics, and popular, humble figures on the margins of society. He made his debut in the 1920s, but it was his post-war movies which set the pace, becoming part of the wave of social realism that was also being expressed in photography. His most famous movies abroad—*Journey to Tokyo* (*Tokyo monogatari*, 1953) and *Equinox Flowers* (*Higanbana*, 1958)—are the symbols of rebirth after the war.

Hirokazu Kore-eda

Ozu's legacy seems to have been passed down to the director Kore-eda (1962), who is enjoying huge international success precisely because of the slow pace of his movies, and meticulous stories about human relationships, starting with *Maborosi* (1995), *Wonderful Life* (1998), and *Distance* (2001), and right up to his three movies about family relationships: *Father and Son* (2013), *After the Storm* (2016), and *Shoplifters* (2018), winner of the Palme d'Or at the Cannes Film Festival.

Epics and Samurai

Many stories recounting the exploits of heroes, bandits, and samurai who fought following the codes of honor, pursuing a sense of justice against corrupt figures and times, were handed down orally and then illustrated and transcribed, first in painted scrolls from the Kamakura period, and later, in the Edo period, in printed illustrated books. There are also many stories that have inspired important movies, showing the world a Japan that

→ Shigeru Ban's public restroom that turns transparent when you come out, part of the *Tokyo Toilet* project in Tokyo's Yoyogi Fukamachi Park

↳ **Japan Through the Eyes of Wim Wenders**
Another movie that deserves a mention is Wim Wenders's *Perfect Days* (2023) and its glimpse into Japanese life through the everyday routine, repetitiveness, and feeling of humility and alienation of a public toilet cleaner in Tokyo. The *Tokyo toilets* in which the story is set were a public architecture project for the city, designed by seventeen contemporary designers and architects, including Fumihiko Maki, Kashiwa Satō, Kengo Kuma, Nao Tamura, Shigeru Ban, Tadao Andō, Toyō Itō, and Sōsuke Fujimoto.

Japan As It Appears in Literature and Films

was still unknown after the war, from *Heike monogatari* to *Suikoden*—a tale imported from China (translated as *Water Margin* in English)—and *Chūshingura*, also adapted to a stage play, which is about forty-seven *rōnin* who perform ritual suicide to avenge their lord and pay homage to him.

The 1954 movie *Godzilla*, directed by Ishirō Hondao and produced by Toho, was a watershed, marking the beginning of the post-war period. It touched the subjects of nuclear weapons and the destruction and metamorphosis immediately after Hiroshima and Nagasaki had been bombed.

From Akira Kurosawa (1910–1998) to Takeshi Kitano

Akira Kurosawa is one of the great directors who were inspired by heroic themes, drawing on both Hollywood and traditional *Nō* theater and laying the foundations of modern Japanese cinema. He made over thirty movies during his career, starting with the 1943 *Sanshiro Sugata*. The 1950 *Rashomon* was revolutionary, but *The Seven Samurai* and *Yojimbo*, released in 1954 and 1961 respectively, also had an international influence on westerns: Sergio Leone's *For a Fistful of Dollars*, for example, but also the *Star Wars* saga, which even in more recent times couldn't ignore Kurosawa's example. As far as Takeshi Kitano is concerned, his training in underground theater and cabaret, as well as his television career as a comedian and anchorman, meant that he was able to add irony, parody, gore, and somber humor to the crime and action dramas he made in the 1980s, about yakuza gangsters and the police. He started out as an actor, then went on to direct *Violent Cop*; in 1993 he produced *Sonatine*, in 1997 he won the Golden Lion in Venice with *Hana-bi*, and in 2003 the Silver Lion with *Zatōichi*, whose humorous irony and musical style inspired foreign directors such as Quentin Tarantino when making his *Kill Bill* saga.

▲ A combat scene from the Japanese film *Rashomon*, directed by Akira Kurosawa, 1950

Dreams and Magic Worlds

While in literature there are the multi-level plots of Haruki Murakami's novels which also use the writer's favorite music as a soundtrack to transport the reader into parallel worlds, music that Murakami then played on his radio show, there are two cinematic masterpieces which shouldn't go unmentioned: *Dreams* (1990) by Kurosawa, and *Dolls* (2002) by Kitano. These two unique works succeeded in recreating a unique poetic and dreamlike dimension, mixing realism and the rawness of life with the theatricality and magic of dreams, through references to traditional theater, the use of costumes and scenery, and music alternating with the silence of the narration.

Manga and Anime: Images of Old and New Worlds

There cannot be a happy ending to the fight between the raging gods and humans. However, even in the middle of hatred and killings, there are things worth living for. A wonderful meeting, or a beautiful thing, can exist. We depict hatred, but it is to depict that there are more important things. We depict a curse, to depict the joy of liberation.

What we should depict is how the boy understands the girl, and the process in which the girl opens her heart to the boy. At the end, the girl will say to the boy "I love you, Ashitaka. But I cannot forgive humans." Smiling, the boy should say "That is fine. Live with me."

— *Hayao Miyazaki, proposing* Mononokehime, *1997*

← Tokyo's Akihabara district, famous for its electronic, video game, manga, cosplay, and anime stores

In recent years, bookstores around the world have multiplied their shelves dedicated to manga, and there is even a museum dedicated to this genre in Kyoto. There are Cosplayer gatherings and fairs in every country, and a new form of tourism has arisen among young generations, generated by the locations mentioned in these comics, and made even more popular by the animated movies and video games based on them.

The classic format of the horizontal scroll paintings (*emaki*) which use long pictorial sequences, sometimes accompanied by calligraphic text, to tell educational and exhilaratingly entertaining stories, started becoming diffused in the Nara period, in order to transmit virtuous examples of Buddhism through anecdotes about the life of Siddhartha and the monks who preached his teachings. Starting in the ninth century, during the Heian period, the ladies of the imperial court started recounting stories about their environment, as well as the customs, combining the protagonists' feelings with descriptions of nature and illustrations of poetic anthologies. During the Kamakura period, with the samurai's rise to power, stories became more epic, with dynamic bloody scenes narrating the battles, clashes, and deeds of generals and heroes. These themes developed even more dynamically in ukiyo-e during the Edo period (1603–1868), thanks to the diffusion of the polychrome printing technique, accelerating the rendering of graphics in genre painting and putting Japan ahead of the rest of the world.

An eleventh-century monk, Toba Sōjō, went down in history for creating a set of scrolls depicting animals performing human tasks, freely drawn in black ink and with humorous features: rabbits, monkeys, foxes, and frogs engaged in religious ceremonies, as priests, worshippers, or Buddha, as well as portraits of them playing games like archery or swimming in a stream. This set of caricatures is known as *Chōjū-jinbutsu-giga*; the scenes move seamlessly from one to another, and this is why the story is generally considered one of the first forms of manga.

▲ Toba Sōjō, *Chōjū jinbutsu giga*, fragment of a scroll, ink painting on paper, 12th–13th century

Hokusai's *Manga*

The word *manga* (漫画) is composed of two characters: *man*, which means "multitude, overflowing, full," but also "free, random, funny, caricatural," and *ga*, or "painting, picture, sketch." The term *manga* came into use in the 18th century, in the Edo period, when ukiyo-e artists started producing popular comic books, *kibyōshi*. However, the best example of contemporary manga is Katsushika Hokusai's series of fifteen volumes titled *Hokusai Manga*, the first of which was published in 1814. They are manuals designed to teach and help those wanting

▲ Katsushika Hokusai, Manga, detail from a page of a volume with sketches of sumo wrestlers, 15 volumes of wood-block prints, from 1814 to 1878

to draw, filled with small sketches to use as models for subjects of all kinds, woodblock-printed in black ink with a few touches of pink.

Twentieth-Century Developments

Kitazawa Rakuten (1876–1955) was the first artist to use the word "manga" in the modern sense, which today indicates all forms of Japanese comics. Manga as we know it today became established in the 1920s, when serialized comic strips appeared in magazines and newspapers. The American occupation during the 1940s and 50s, following Japan's defeat in World War II, marked a significant turning point in graphic production, with the introduction of American animations and a style inspired by the *kasutori* magazines printed on uncoated paper with bright, colorful graphics. After years of deprivation and destruction, even chocolate bars, cigarette packets, and cans of American food rations were seized upon as an artistic stimulus.

In Osaka, the trend of printing fairy tales in cheaply made booklets emerged—known as "red books" (*akahon*)—to be sold in street stalls. The most successful was *Shin Takarajima (Treasure Island)*, created in 1947 by Osamu Tezuka (1928–1989) and Sakai Shichima (1905–1969), the fathers of modern Japanese manga.

There were two manga series made into anime which definitively influenced the history of the genre: Osamu Tezuka's *Mighty Atom* (known as *Astro Boy* in the United States and the West), which began in April 1951, and Machiko Hasegawa's *Sazae-san*, started in April 1946.

The *Shōjo* Genre

Japan's two main manga genres developed in the 1950s and 60s: *Shōnen*, aimed at teenage boys, and *Shōjo*, aimed at girls. The protagonists of the latter are strong, independent female characters with intense emotions, which are expressed, together with their experiences, through delicate, graceful drawings.

In 1969, a group of artists—later called the Year 24 Group or The Magnificent Forty-Niners—debuted in the *shōjo* genre, marking the first major entry of female artists into the manga world, which has since become dominated by female *mangaka* who draw for a young female audience.

In 1972, Ikeda launched the extremely famous *shōjo* manga series *Berusaiyu no Bara (The Rose of Versailles)*, known worldwide for the animated version Lady Oscar, a story that challenged Japan's neo-Confucian principles which defined women's roles and activities. The protagonist was Oscar François de Jarjayes, a female captain of the guards at Marie Antoinette's palace in pre-revolutionary France. In the nineties, Naoko Takeuchi designed *Bishōjo senshi Sērāmūn*, which is *Sailor Moon*, one of the best-selling *shōjo* series of all time, released in eighteen pocket volumes and one of the most watched animated series in the world.

Alongside the increase in female readers, the *shōjo* genre evolved into subgenres: *josei,* or Ladies' Comics, which deal with topics such as work, emotions, sexual relationships, friendships and female relationships; *oshare*, or fashion manga, such as *Paradise Kiss* by Ai Yazawa; horror-vampire-gothic, like *Vampire Knight* by Matsuri Hino; and several others.

The *Shōnen* Genre

Mangas for male readers are classified according to the age of the audience: those for boys up to eighteen years old are called *shōnen manga*, those for young people up to thirty are known as *seinen manga*.

Since the 1950s, *shōnen mangas* have focused on topics that are considered masculine, all about technology and science fiction, such as robots and space travel, and heroic action adventures. The first stories were often about putting abilities to the test, designed to be educational, and self-discipline, going as far as sacrificing oneself for the cause in the name of society, the community, and family. *Astro Boy* by Tezuka and *Doraemon* by Fujiko F. Fujio are early examples of stories about robots.

Fantasy and historical military mangas about heroic warriors and martial artists are also extremely popular. Some can be very serious, such as Sanpei Shirato's *Kamui den (The Legend of Kamui)* and Nobuhiro Watsuki's *Rurouni Kenshin (Rurouni Kenshin: Meiji Swordsman Romantic Story)*; others also contain humorous elements, like Akira Toriyama's *Doragon Bōru (Dragon Ball)*. In addition to the above-mentioned subgenres, there is no shortage of sports manga and anime for both men and

↑ Monkey D. Luffy, protagonist of the anime *One Piece*, exhibited in a Jump manga store in Tokyo

women, such as Inazuma and Eleven. One of the most successful manga series worth mentioning is *Wan Pīsu (ONE PIECE)*, which has been going since 1997 and is expected to end by 2025. The protagonist is a boy with a rubber-like body, who travels the world on a pirate ship in search of priceless treasure.

Anime: the Greatest Series

The first Japanese animation studios began establishing themselves in the 1950s. The Nihon Dōga Eiga studio was founded in 1948 and renamed Toei Dōga in 1956. It produced the most famous anime, including *Tiger Man*, *Mazinga Z*, *Captain Harlock*, and *Sailor Moon*, while in 1963 Tezuka Osamu premiered *Astro Boy* on Fuji TV, and it became the first anime series watched by the general public in the West to influence American popular culture, and all subsequent anime about robots and space.

▲ Life-size figures of the adorable cat Doraemon, protagonist of anime and manga, on the roof of the Tokyo Tower Foot Town during the Fujiko Fujio exhibition

In the 1970s, television series made their mark. One of the first productions was *Lupin III*, followed by *Arupusu no shōjo Haiji (Heidi, Girl of the Alps)* by Isao Takahata in 1974.

The latter was so successful internationally that it permitted Hayao Miyazaki and Takahata to start a series of anime based on literature.

Two of Miyazaki's most critically acclaimed productions in that decade were *Mirai shōnen Konan (Future Boy Conan*, 1978), and *Rupan Sansei: Kariosutoro no shiro (Lupin III: The Castle of Cagliostro*, 1979).

During this period, Japanese animated children's series arrived in continental Europe; in addition to the well-known *Barbapapa*, *Vicky the Viking*, and *The Rose of Versailles*, there were also mecha anime such as *Mazinga Z* (1972–74), *Gatchaman* (1972–74), *Space Battleship Yamato* (1974–75) and *Mobile Fighter G Gundam* (1979–80), which were also made into movies.

→ Kaonashi, a character in the animated film *Spirited Away* by Studio Ghibli, during a preview of Ghibli Park in Nagakute

Studio Ghibli

Driven by the success of *Nausicaä of the Valley of the Wind*, in 1985 Hayao Miyazaki, Isao Takahata, Toshio Suzuki, and Yasuyoshi Tokuma founded the Studio Ghibli, and over time they created several Japanese animation masterpieces, including: *Laputa—Castle in the Sky* (1986), *My Neighbor Totoro* (1988), *Kiki's Delivery Service* (1989), *Porco Rosso* (1992), *Princess Mononoke* (1997), *Spirited Away* (2001), *Howl's Moving Castle* (2004), and *The Boy and the Heron* (2023). The studio skillfully created a universe of colors, characters, and stories in which human and mechanical beings, good and evil, and the earthly world and the celestial realm are not separated, but rather slide into each other, imbued with that sense of animism that permeates all Japanese culture.

↑ Dondoko Forest from the animated film *My Neighbor Totoro*, during a preview of Ghibli Park in Nagakute

Cosplay and Manga Cafes

Costume play, or dressing up and acting like famous characters in movies, cartoons, comics, and video games at festivals, is now widespread throughout the world.

The term was coined by the Japanese journalist Takahashi in the 1970s, while the first cosplay contest was held at the World Science Fiction Convention in Los Angeles in 1984.

Alongside this craze, manga cafes, or *mangakissa* (*kissa* is the abbreviation of *kissaten*, which means bar or cafeteria), popped up throughout Japan. These are places where you can enjoy a drink while reading manga, but there are also video games, televisions, vending machines for snacks and drinks, and often those who don't have a place to sleep at night, or cannot afford to pay a fixed rent, choose to rent a booth in one.

→ A couple of Cosplayers, or anime fans, at the convention at Tokyo Big Sight

Manga and Anime: Images of Old and New Worlds

The Other Face of Japan: *Pachinko* and *Karaoke*

While you're playing yourself out in lonesome dissipation in front of a pinball machine, someone else might be reading through Proust. Still another might be engaged in heavy petting with a girlfriend [...]. The one could well become a writer [...]; the others, a happily married couple. [...] Pinball machines, however, won't lead you anywhere.

— Haruki Murakami, Wind/Pinball

There is another side to Japan that seems alien to the Japan known for its cherry blossoms, high-quality craftsmanship, fine food, and *omotenashi*—that sense of heartfelt hospitality that everyone who comes to this country appreciates as one of the qualities that makes a difference. It is marked by a mixture of endless hours at work and entertainment in places where people tend to compulsively de-stress, or at least relieve stress, such as *izakaya, karaoke, pachinko,* and video game arcades. And there are also alternative life choices that go against homologation, with an underground nightlife scene of jazz and singular passions, found in hidden bars and alleys.

← *Pachinko* arcade in the Akihabara district in Tokyo

The best place to start if we want to better understand Japanese society is with the two Chinese characters that define the concept of *uchi*, "inside," and *soto*, "outside." Unlike Western societies, which glorify individualism, in Japan—and in Asia generally—the value system is based on the group, on belonging to it and on safeguarding it. As well as absorbing China's Buddhist philosophy, Japan also absorbed Confucianism, building a society with a class system based on the principle of filial piety, or respect for the elderly and superiors; on the sense of duty, which prevails over personal feelings; on the importance of the community one belongs to, starting with family and followed by school; sports or music clubs; one's company; and ultimately the homeland.

In concrete terms, this is expressed by the homogenization of thinking and behavior within the group, which leads, for example, to a bottom-up decision-making system within companies that is conflict-free; it leads to people giving positive answers even when they think otherwise, to spending their little free time in the evening—and often even holidays—in the company of work colleagues instead of with family or friends.

In contemporary society, the service and dedication that a younger person with a lower rank gives their superior, which in the era of the Shoguns was a samurai's moral code of loyalty and respect (*bushidō*) toward their general—so much so that not having a master became a stigma of the *rōnin* samurai—can especially be seen within companies where there is still the unhealthy habit of working without limits, because it is unthinkable for a person to leave the workplace before their superior, even when they have finished; and if their boss asks them to, they have to accept spending time with colleagues, at the expense of their own free time.

↟ Employees going home after work in Tokyo

Suicide

Suicide in Japan is one of the most discussed and misunderstood topics in the West; and it is not easy to define it, given the completely different cultural premises.

Ancient sources often refer to ritual suicide, like *seppuku* or *harakiri*. It was a samurai's ultimate expression of honor and loyalty toward his general and his clan, or that of lovers whose love for each other (*ninjō*) could not find fulfillment on earth in the context of social conventions (*giri*).

In wartime, *kamikaze* pilots embodied the absolute principle of honor

Curiosity

◂ In the 1970s, a reportage on the Japanese industrial and educational model was published in the magazine "Epoca," in the context of the dramatic modernization in preparation for the first international event, the Osaka Expo. The photos portrayed company employees venting their **anger** and **resentment** by hitting a large doll of their boss with canes. The doll was placed in a corner, and feelings of disapproval were channeled into an action that was socially controlled by the company-family.

suicide by sacrificing themselves for the homeland, in the name of the emperor.

A form of sacred suicide among Buddhist monks is well-documented: to conclude his ascetic path, a hermit monk would retreat into a cave in the woods and fast until he died, thereby becoming a *sokushinbutsu*.

Today these practices are banned, but the increase in suicides (*jisatsu*) recorded among young people due to professional stress (*karōjisatsu*), and deaths from overworking (*karōshi*), is one of the ongoing social problems related to an economic and social system that has given rise to a distorted world of work, to relationships based on the silent obligation (*giri*) to adapt to the group under penalty of exclusion: all this is starting to falter, leading to "recluses" who cannot find a balance between themselves and the category they belong to.

Hikikomori

This compound word literally means "withdraw, remove" (from the verb *hiku*) and "hide oneself, seclude oneself" (from the verb *komoru*).

↑ A *hikikomori* shut inside his room

The word is commonly used to indicate a bat, but since the eighties the term has taken on a social connotation with reference to the increasingly widespread phenomenon of young people who end up closing themselves alone in their rooms, abandoning real private and public relationships to only live through indirect social relationships.

This behavior reveals problems with social integration, and is often linked to forms of depression and obsessive-compulsive disorders; the problem becomes evident when there is sudden absenteeism at school or work, where the pressure to perform and compete is sometimes no longer bearable and leads to burnout.

Places of Perdition
Pachinko

Just walking past the open door of a pachinko arcade is a mind-blowing experience, due to the deafening sound of the music coming from the slot and pinball machines. Every morning, even before the shops and offices open, people of all ages and genders are often seen queueing outside, sitting on their heels or standing with a mobile phone in their hand, waiting to get inside and play.

Playing is simple: inserting a coin into the machine releases a number of steel balls, which must then be launched using a spring lever, in the hope that they will land in one of the holes. The holes are worth different numbers of points; and the more points you score, the more balls you win. The player is passive while playing *pachinko*: apart from controlling the speed with which the steel balls are launched into the machine, they spend their time hypnotized by the way they move, the colorful lights, and the deafening noise around them.

The balls can be exchanged for products or cash at any time, at a small window found outside the arcade, away from the gambling machines.

The origins of *pachinko* can be traced back to the 1920s, when Japanese inventors began experimenting with mechanical games inspired by the popular pinball machine. These early machines, known as *korinto gashi*, were manual devices that shot small metal balls into a mechanism with scores. *Pachinko* as we know it today began to take shape in the 1930s, evolving with the addition of flashing lights, sound effects, and, in the 1960s, even electrically operated bumpers. Electronic machines were introduced in the 1980s, followed by digital displays, but *pachinko* continues to be one of the most alienating places in Japan, and they are still part of the popular urban landscape near stations, or inside shopping malls.

→ A group of friends having fun singing in a *karaoke* room

Karaoke

The word karaoke is a combination of the Chinese character *kara*, "empty," and the Japanese phonetic character *oke*, the abbreviation of *okesutora*, or "orchestra." The word therefore means "empty orchestra." Karaoke as a form of entertainment was invented in the second half of the 1960s, when the patrons of a bar were made to sing popular songs which everyone could listen to, using a microphone connected to an eight-track tape player. The first karaoke prototype, called the Sparko Box, was designed by the engineer Shigeichi Negishi in 1967; the singers were provided with a booklet containing the lyrics of the songs they had to sing. In 1970,

The Other Face of Japan: Pachinko and Karaoke

Toshiharu Yamashita, a singing teacher, used this system for practicing, but the key figure in making the phenomenon popular was the musician Daisuke Inoue. In 1971 he invested in the production of the coin-operated 8-Juke machine, which—for a fee—provided a few minutes of amplified instrumental singing with reverb effects, and he put them in bars in the Kobe area. Since then, karaoke has been one of the most loved forms of entertainment, and the Japanese use it to socialize, to get to know each other, to form a group, and also to draw in foreign customers, creating an intimate atmosphere that overcomes any language barriers. This all takes place in dedicated venues, where you can book your own room with a TV and sofas, and have a relaxing drink. However, there is also the phenomenon of solo karaoke (*hitokara*), where people go to practice singing in the hope of making it into a profession.

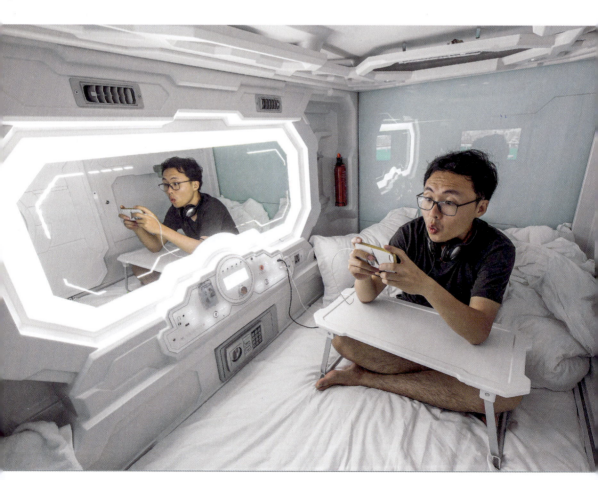

Sometimes you can hear drunken singing or elegant, trained voices drifting out of half-open windows as you walk through the alleys of certain neighborhoods which in the past were known for their popular culture and alternative artistic nightlife scene, where tiny bars and establishments hidden behind mysterious doors or at the bottom of eerie staircases only have room for four or five patrons at a time. The Golden Gai district in Tokyo, featured in Wim Wenders's movie *Tokyo Ga*, and Pontochō in Kyoto, frequented by actors, directors, and artists, still offer this type of experience, albeit invaded by tourism, which has radically transformed its secret atmosphere.

Capsule Hotels

For Japanese *sarari man* (salarymen) who miss the last train home, often to the suburbs, after a night of fun in the traditional *izakaya* taverns, karaoke venues, or clubs, and have to find accommodation for a few hours until the first train at five in the morning, or until they have to go to work, there are capsule hotels. They are one of the most fascinating, avant-garde, and futuristic inventions of the 1970s, launched in Osaka in the wake of Expo '70 to solve the problem of daily routine. You can find accommodation in a compact capsule with a TV at the same price as a train ticket. They measure about 2 x 1 meters, and are inserted into a wall with several floors, often with separate areas for males and females, making them safer also for traveling tourists to use.

◀ A boy relaxing in a *capsule hotel* cabin

Hiroshima, Nagasaki and Fukushima

[…] when I started taking photographs of the victims, they willingly stood in front of my camera, with the sincere hope that my photographs would help prevent other Japanese people from falling victim to atomic bombs like they had. […] I took so many photos with tears in my eyes!

— *Ken Domon*, Hiroshima, Kenkōsha, *Tokyo, 1958*

← The Hiroshima Dome is the symbol of the destruction and reconstruction of the city of Hiroshima after the explosion of the atomic bomb in 1945, and the heart of the Peace Memorial Park

Throughout history, the Japanese archipelago has repeatedly suffered major catastrophes related to the volcanic and seismic nature of the area. On top of these phenomena there is also the power of the ocean, which produces the tsunamis that sometimes occur following more powerful seismic events, destroying the coastal areas, and extreme weather events, with torrential rains and typhoons that are a particular threat to the southern islands in summer. Other catastrophic events that have affected Japan were instead due to human choices, such as the two atomic bombs dropped on Hiroshima and Nagasaki in 1945, and the nuclear disaster at Fukushima in 2011.

August 6 and August 9, 1945, are two dates that mark a point of no return in the history of humanity. The American air force dropped atomic bombs on the Japanese cities of Hiroshima and Nagasaki, tragically ending the Second World War that had already devastated the archipelago with years of bombing.

Hiroshima and Nagasaki

Emperor Hirohito's radio speech announcing Japan's unconditional surrender revealed the huge deception of war propaganda to the population, putting an end to the imperial and imperialist myth and to the State Shintoism that had formed the foundation of militarist ideology.

The powerful atomic explosion that hit Hiroshima at 8:15 am on August 6, 1945, caused by a uranium bomb dropped by the American B-29 bomber *Enola Gay* and captured by the images of the large mushroom cloud that covered the city, destroyed ninety percent of Hiroshima's buildings. In a split second, more than half of the population died, burned to death by the heat of the explosion, and thousands more died not only days later from their injuries, but also from radiation exposure months and years later.

This "hell on earth," as the *hibakusha* (survivors) call it, is also evidenced by the many melted, deformed, and burned objects—today mostly preserved in the Hiroshima Peace Museum—and the silhouettes of people etched in stone, like freeze-frames.

Three days later, on August 9, Nagasaki, a historically major port city for foreign trade, was hit by a plutonium bomb at 11:02 am, dropped by the American bomber *Fat Man*. It is said that there were about eighty thousand victims, in a city with a thriving Christian community and many steel and arms works, such as Mitsubishi.

▲ A photo of the mushroom cloud that rose after the atomic bomb was dropped on Hiroshima on August 6, 1945

A pocket watch without hands found in Hiroshima, photographed by Ken Domon, and a wristwatch with its hands frozen at 11:02 am, the time the bomb hit Nagasaki, photographed by Shōmei Tōmatsu, are emblems of the moment time stopped.

The Memory Theme

The Hiroshima Dome is the most important building in the city. After the atomic bomb, its remains were left standing in memory of what had happened, and the steel frame was all that was left of the dome. At the time of the bombing, it was the Hiroshima Prefectural Industrial Promotion Hall, and it overlooks the Motoyasu River, right opposite the Aioi Bridge, which was the bomb's target. It was recognized as a UNESCO World Heritage Site in 1996.

Today it is the heart of what is now the Hiroshima Peace Memorial Park (Heiwa Kinen Kōen), designed by architect Kenzō Tange, home to

▲ Lanterns lit every August to commemorate the dead and invoke peace in the Hiroshima Peace Memorial Park

the Museum of Peace, which contains photos, objects completely deformed by the heat of the explosion, and the testimonies of the *hibakusha*, those who survived to recount their experience (*kataribe*), and who play a role in raising awareness. Then there is the monument dedicated to Sadako Sasaki, a little girl who was two years old when the atomic bomb hit, and who got leukemia due to radiation. She promised to fold a thousand origami cranes but died on October 25, 1955.

Every year, in memory of Sadako and her fight to live, thousands of origami crane necklaces are donated from all over the world and kept in large glass cases. They are regularly recycled to produce objects related to the message of peace. Finally, there is the Cenotaph for the victims, a large concrete sculpture that opens toward the sky like two wings or two hands, aligned with the Peace Arch, where a flame has been burning in memory of the victims since 1964.

→ Every year, origami cranes (*orizuru*) are donated to the Sadako Sasaki Monument in Hiroshima Peace Memorial Park from around the world, as a prayer

152   Japan

Hiroshima by Ken Domon

The master photographer of realism recorded his first visit to Hiroshima in his notebook on July 23, 1957, at 2:40 pm. It was a journey that changed his life because he realized that he didn't know anything about what had really happened in Hiroshima, or what it had meant. He went there six times, for a total of thirty-six days, and between July and November he took almost eight thousand negatives; images that no one would then want to see, and which caused a scandal when some of them were printed in the book *Hiroshima* (1958); a larger collection later appeared in the book *Living Hiroshima* (*Ikiteiru Hiroshima*, 1978).

Thirteen years after the atomic bomb was dropped on Hiroshima, the work once again drew the world's attention to the open, yet forgotten, wounds of the residents, producing a strong social backlash in Hiroshima, Nagasaki, and Fukushima.

Information on the effects of the atomic bomb in fact continued to be fragmentary, at times completely absent, censored, or silenced by both the American occupation forces and the Japanese government itself.

Photographs, drawings, poems, and writings attesting to the disasters caused by the bomb could only be published freely after 1951, the year of the San Francisco Peace Treaty. These included the 1952 August 6 issue of the weekly magazine *Asahi Graphic,* which published some photographs of the disasters caused in Nagasaki and Hiroshima; the images shocked readers all over Japan, so much so that it could be said it was the first time they had found out what had really happened. One hundred and eighty photos taken with his 35 mm camera, through which Domon coldly and horrifically—because that was the reality—recorded both the material and moral damages, children in orphanages suffering physical and psychological problems due to their mothers' exposure to radiation, the deep scars, the plastic-surgery operations and transplants the victims of the bomb underwent, dedicating precisely to the progress of medicine in this field, the fourteen pages at the beginning of the volume, which became a true photographic dossier.

Hiroshima was therefore not only about those who died in 1945, but also about the living, who continued to struggle years later. Thanks to this new retrospective, *Hiroshima* marked a turning point in the history of post-war art, getting to the heart of reality at that time, and being the first contemporary work to obtain the Mainichi Photography Award, in 1958, and then Photographer of the Year Award from the Japan Photo Critics Association.

The Great East Japan Earthquake

On March 11, 2011, a magnitude 9 earthquake was felt throughout the country, the strongest in Japan's recorded history, followed by an extraordinary tsunami with waves over 98 feet (30 meters) high, which hit the Tōhoku region on the northeastern coast. Not only was this event a natural catastrophe that put a strain on the resilience of the local Japanese population, but it was also a terrible warning to the entire world.

The consequences of the damage to the Fukushima nuclear power plant's generators and the cooling system of three reactors, with the resulting dispersion of radioactive materials in the ocean and danger of explosion, revealed the fragility and limits of such delicate, necessary, and destructive structures, dependent on human management.

The most affected prefectures were Iwate and Miyagi, with almost twenty thousand dead and over two thousand five hundred people missing. Over one hundred and twenty thousand homes were destroyed, evacuated, or rendered unusable in the entire area around Fukushima. Fishing was banned and livestock farms destroyed or put down due to radiation making meat, vegetables, and derivatives inedible.

Creativity and Memory

The Tōhoku region is renowned for its mountains, greenery, hot springs, good food, and local artisans skilled in metallurgy and woodworking, using wood from the wooded areas which are covered with snow for many months. It had never been considered important from a creative and artistic point of view—

Bibliography and filmography

- **Masuji Ibuse**, *Black Rain*, Kodansha International (2012). The book was adapted into a film directed by Shōhei Imamura, *Black Rain (Kuroi ame)*, 1989.
- **Kenzaburō Ōe**, *Hiroshima Notes*, Grove Press, 1996.
- **Rossella Menegazzo and Takeshi Fujimori** (editor), with the help of Yuki Seli, *Domon Ken. The Master of Japanese Realism*, Skira, Milan 2016.
- **Ken Domon**, *Hiroshima*, Kenkōsha, Tokyo 1958
- **Shōmei Tōmatsu**, *<11:02> Nagasaki*, 1966
- **Shōmei Tōmatsu, Ken Domon**, *Hiroshima—Nagasaki Document 1961*, The Japan Council Against A & H Bombs, Tokyo 1961

▲ Images of the devastation caused by the earthquake and tsunami of March 11, 2011, on the northeastern coastal region of Tōhoku

that is, until the destructive events of 2011 brought the intangible and artisanal heritage of these areas back to the center of national debates. Designers, architects, photographers, filmmakers, and curators have somehow rediscovered the region's qualities, by providing their skills to valorize and revive small local businesses, also attracting national and international audiences. A group of designers, architects, and curators together with a sushi chef from Tōhoku created the collaborative Ishinomaki Kobo project to support the population, which has now become a DIY furniture brand. The 2011 edition of the Yamagata International Documentary Film Festival screened an incredible twenty-nine documentaries filmed by professional and amateur filmmakers during the earthquake and tsunami; over the following years, this category became a section in the festival. In 2012, the 21_21 Design Sight space in Tokyo hosted an exhibition on design, craftsmanship, and local traditions entitled *Tohoku no Temahima* (The Art of Living in Tōhoku). The Japan Pavilion at the two Venice Biennials of Architecture (2012) and Art (2013), proposed installations and projects created with recycled materials from the areas affected by the earthquake: the first, *Architecture in the wake of disaster*, curated by Toyo Ito; the second, *Statement for abstract speaking—Sharing uncertainty and collective acts*, curated by Mika Kuraya and Koki Tanak.

↳ Alongside human lives and homes, hundreds of thousands of family photographs, stories, and personal memories were lost in the mud. The project "Tsunami, Photographs and Then" *Family Photos Swept Away by 3.11 East Japan Tsunami*, launched on Twitter by professor Shibata of Ostuma Women's University with the aim of finding, cleaning, and returning lost photos and memories to their rightful owners, attracted hundreds of volunteers. By 2014, with the help of firefighters, the police, and photographer Munemasa Takahashi, they had recovered, digitized, filed, and returned about four hundred thousand of seven hundred and fifty thousand photos, which they then published in a photobook.

Rossella Menegazzo

Rossella Menegazzo is an associate professor of East Asian Art History at the University of Milan, and author of many publications. She also organizes conferences and curates exhibitions on Japanese art and culture, collaborating with the most important international museum institutions. In 2017, she received the Japan Ministry of Foreign Affairs award for the "promotion of Japanese culture in Italy".

Captions for the photos in the middle of the book:

pp. 74–75 A Shinto priest beats a drum (*taikō*) during the ceremony at the Meiji Shrine

p. 76 A woman accompanying two girls dressed in kimonos to the shrine for *Shichi-Go-San*, the festival for children aged 3 (*san*), 5 (*go*), and 7 (*shichi*), celebrated annually on November 15 to pray for their good health and well-being

p. 77 Tokyo is the cradle of the street fashion and vintage clothes which also influenced high fashion

pp. 78–79 Crowds of picnickers by the Togetsu bridge in Arashiyama (Kyoto) admiring the cherry blossoms (*hanami*)

p. 80 A girl dressed in home-made vintage clothes at a bus stop in Tokyo

p. 81 A little girl in a kimono going to the shrine for the *Shichi-Go-San* festival

pp. 82–83 A man going home after work through Tokyo's streets lined with illuminated skyscrapers

pp. 84–85 Japanese flower-shaped candy (*wagashi*), reminiscent of the colors and shapes of the seasons

pp. 86–87 Skyscrapers lit up with advertising billboards in the Akihabara district of Tokyo, famous for its arcades and video-game stores

p. 88 Utagawa Hiroshige, *In the Mountains of Izu Province*, from the series *Thirty-six Views of Mount Fuji*, polychrome wood-block print, 1858

p. 89 Lake Ashi with the shrine's sacred Shinto entrance gate (*torii*). In the background, Mount Fuji

p. 90 A plate of Japanese *nerikiri* candy with a bowl of powdered green tea (*maccha*)

p. 91 Tōshūsai Sharaku, *The Actor Ichikawa Danjuro VI as Arakawa Taro Takesada*, polychrome wood-block print, 1794

Iconographic references

p. 2 Stuart Freedman/Corbis Historical/Getty Images
p. 5 Heritage Images/Hulton Archive/Getty Images
p. 8 Prisma by Dukas/Universal Images Group/Getty Images
p. 13 The Metropolitan Museum of Art, New York, Rogers Fund, 1925 (Open Access)
p. 14 Werner Forman/Universal Images Group/Getty Images
p. 15 GraphicaArtis/Archive Photos/Getty Images
p. 17 John S Lander/LightRocket/Getty Images
p. 18 Heritage Images/Hulton Archive/Getty Images
p. 22 Carl Court/Getty Images News/Getty Images
p. 23 Indianapolis Museum of Art at Newfields/Archive Photos/Getty Images
p. 24 Heritage Images/Hulton Archive/Getty Images
p. 26 Farzan Bilimoria/Moment Mobile/Getty Images
p. 27 Sepia Times/Universal Images Group/Getty Images
pp. 28-29 The Metropolitan Museum of Art, New York, Rogers Fund, 1922 (Open Access)
p. 30 Elizabeth Beard/Moment/Getty Images
p. 33 Pictures from History/Universal Images Group/Getty Images
p. 35 Heritage Images/Hulton Archive/Getty Images
p. 38 Heritage Images/Hulton Archive/Getty Images
p. 40 Stuart Freedman/Corbis Historical/Getty Images
p. 43 Sepia Times/Universal Images Group/Getty Images
p. 44 Masashi Hara/Getty Images Sport/Getty Images
p. 46 Marco Montalti/iStock/Getty Images
p. 47 Panther Media GmbH / Alamy Stock Photo
p. 48 John S Lander/LightRocket/Getty Images
pp. 50-51 Frédéric Soltan/Corbis News/Getty Images
p. 52 Werner Forman/Universal Images Group/Getty Images

p. 56 Sepia Times /Universal Images Group/Getty Images
p. 57 Werner Forman/Universal Images Group/Getty Images
p. 59 Print Collector/Hulton Archive/Getty Images
p. 61 The Asahi Shimbun/Getty Images
p. 62 ome pianuch/Shutterstock
p. 65 John S Lander/LightRocket/Getty Images
p. 67 Alf Hall/Shutterstock
p. 68 EQRoy/Shutterstock
p. 70 aomas/Shutterstock
p. 71 Connie Carolline/Shutterstock
pp. 72-73 Christopher Pillitz/Hulton Archive/Getty Images
pp. 74-75 Eye Ubiquitous/Universal Images Group/Getty Images
p. 76 John S Lander/LightRocket/Getty Images
p. 77 Onnie A Koski/Getty Images Entertainment/Getty Images
pp. 78-79 The Asahi Shimbu/Getty Images
p. 80 Matthew Sperzel/Getty Images Entertainment/Getty Images
p. 81 John S Lander/LightRocket/Getty Images
pp. 82-83 Chris McGrath/Getty Images News/Getty Images
pp. 84-85 owngarden/Moment/Getty Images
pp. 86-87 JC MILHET/AFP/Getty Images
p. 88 Pictures from History/Universal Images Group/Getty Images
p. 89 Prisma by Dukas/Universal Images Group/Getty Images
p. 90 Kwang Meena/Shutterstock
p. 91 Sepia Times/Universal Images Group/Getty Images
p. 92 PYMCA/Avalon/Hulton Archive/Getty Images
p. 95 John S Lander/LightRocket/Getty Images
p. 97 Nataliya Hora / Alamy Stock Photo
p. 99 YOSHIKAZU TSUNO/AFP/Getty Images
p. 101 Aflo Co. Ltd. / Alamy Stock Photo
p. 102 Onnie A Koski/Getty Images Entertainment/Getty Images
p. 104 Manuel Ascanio/Shutterstock
p. 107 View Pictures/Universal Images Group/Getty Images
p. 109 Education Images/Universal Images Group/Getty Images
p. 110 South China Morning Post/Getty Images
p. 111 South China Morning Post/Getty Images
p. 113 Marc GANTIER/Gamma-Rapho/Getty Images
p. 114 Kyodo News/Getty Images
p. 115 Kyodo News/Getty Images
p. 116 Derek Hudson/Hulton Archive/Getty Images
p. 119 Heritage Images/Hulton Archive/Getty Images
p. 120 Leonardo Cendamo/Hulton Archive/Getty Images
p. 123 Carl Court/Getty Images Entertainment/Getty Images
p. 125 Hulton Archive/Getty Images
p. 126 Education Images/Universal Images Group/Getty Images
p. 129 Burstein Collection/Corbis Historical/Getty Images
p. 130 Fine Art/Corbis Historical/Getty Images
p. 133 BEHROUZ MEHRI/AFP/Getty Images
p. 134 TORU YAMANAKA /AFP/Getty Images
p. 135 Tomohiro Ohsumi/Getty Images News/Getty Images
p. 136 Tomohiro Ohsumi/Getty Images News/Getty Images
p. 137 Kurita KAKU/Gamma-Rapho/Getty Images
p. 138 Prisma by Dukas/Universal Images Group/Getty Images
p. 141 Taro Karibe/Getty Images News/Getty Images
p. 143 Aflo Co., Ltd. / Alamy Stock Photo
p. 145 a-clip/Getty Images
p. 146 Jimmy Yan/Shutterstock
p. 148 Junko Kimura/Getty Images News/Getty Images
p. 151 Junko Kimura/Getty Images News/Getty Images
p. 152 Junko Kimura/Getty Images News/Getty Images
p. 153 Junko Kimura/Getty Images News/Getty Images
p. 156 Satoshi Takahashi/LightRocket/Getty Images
p. 157 YASUYOSHI CHIBA/AFP/Getty Images

Acknowledgments

One book is not nearly enough to cover some of the concepts necessary to go beyond that first exotic fascination for a culture that is so peculiar, and distant from the values of Western cultures. And yet the hope is that every traveler will find at least one interesting subject matter in this book, one that inspires them, resonates with them, and leads them to further research and journeys. The wide variety of subjects touched upon deserve just as many acknowledgments, to both the famous and lesser-known people encountered on the journey that led me here. Therefore, I will limit myself to thanking the entire editorial staff for their patience and dedication in completing this project, and Eleonora Lanza and Takayuki Seri for their help in researching more specific topics.

Concept and Editorial Project
Balthazar Pagani / BesideBooks

Graphic Design and Layout
Bebung

Photo Research
William Dello Russo

WS whitestar™ is a trademark property of White Star s.r.l.

© 2024 White Star s.r.l.
Piazzale Luigi Cadorna, 6
20123 Milan, Italy
www.whitestar.it

Translation: Qontent
Editing: Phillip Gaskill

All rights reserved. No part of this publication may be reproduced, stored in a retrieval system, or transmitted in any form or by any means, electronic, mechanical, photocopying, recording, or otherwise, without written permission from the publisher.

ISBN 978-88-544-2082-3
1 2 3 4 5 6   28 27 26 25 24

Printed in China